LIVES OF GREAT RELIGIOUS BOOKS

The *Bhagavad Gita*

LIVES OF GREAT RELIGIOUS BOOKS

FORTHCOMING:

The *Bhagavad Gita*

A BIOGRAPHY

Richard H. Davis

PRINCETON UNIVERSITY PRESS

Princeton and Oxford

Copyright © 2015 by Princeton University Press
Published by Princeton University Press, 41 William Street,
Princeton, New Jersey 08540
In the United Kingdom: Princeton University Press, 6 Oxford Street,
Woodstock, Oxfordshire OX20 1TW

press.princeton.edu

Jacket illustration © B. G. Sharma. www.bgsharmaart.com

Library of Congress Cataloging-in-Publication Data

Davis, Richard H., 1951–
     The Bhagavad Gita : a biography / Richard H. Davis.
          pages cm — (Lives of great religious books)
     Summary: "The Bhagavad Gita, perhaps the most famous of all Indian
scriptures, is universally regarded as one of the world's spiritual and literary
masterpieces. Richard Davis tells the story of this venerable and enduring
book, from its origins in ancient India to its reception today as a spiritual
classic that has been translated into more than seventy-five languages. The
Gita opens on the eve of a mighty battle, when the warrior Arjuna is over-
whelmed by despair and refuses to fight. He turns to his charioteer,
Krishna, who counsels him on why he must. In the dialogue that follows,
Arjuna comes to realize that the true battle is for his own soul. Davis highlights the place of this legendary dialogue in classical Indian culture, and
then examines how it has lived on in diverse settings and contexts. He looks
at the medieval devotional traditions surrounding the divine character of
Krishna and traces how the Gita traveled from India to the West, where it
found admirers in such figures as Ralph Waldo Emerson, Henry David
Thoreau, J. Robert Oppenheimer, and Aldous Huxley. Davis explores how
Indian nationalists like Mahatma Gandhi and Swami Vivekananda used
the Gita in their fight against colonial rule, and how contemporary interpreters reanimate and perform this classical work for audiences today. An
essential biography of a timeless masterpiece, this book is an ideal introduction to the Gita and its insights into the struggle for self-mastery that we all
must wage"— Provided by publisher.
     Includes bibliographical references and index.
     ISBN 978-0-691-13996-8 (hardback)
     1. Bhagavadgita—History. 2. Bhagavadgita—Criticism, interpretation,
etc. I. Title.
     BL1138.66.D38 2014
     294.5'92409—dc23
     2014023890

British Library Cataloging-in-Publication Data is available

This book has been composed in Garamond Premier Pro

Printed on acid-free paper.

Printed in the United States of America

10 9 8 7 6 5 4 3 2 1

CONTENTS

ILLUSTRATIONS

ACKNOWLEDGMENTS

I am grateful to Fred Appel for asking me to work on a biography of the *Bhagavad Gita*. His invitation set me on a journey that has been challenging and rewarding, and it is not over yet.

In the course of my work on this biography, I've profited from the conversations, enthusiasm, and suggestions of many friends and colleagues. At Bard College, my colleagues Sanjib Baruah, Bruce Chilton, and Carolyn Dewald all read portions of this work and gave valuable comments. Kristin Scheible read through a full draft of the manuscript with her class on "Reading Religious Texts," to see how well it would work as an undergraduate course book. I appreciate the comments and advice of Dennis Dalton, Joshua Greene, Brian Hatcher, Jack Hawley, Gene Irschick, Jon Keune, Steve Lindquist, Donald Lopez, Christian Novetzke, Phil Oldenberg, Rosane Rocher, Steve Rosen, Gordon Stavig, and Tom Trautmann on various portions of this work. I am also grateful for the thoughtful suggestions of the anonymous readers at Princeton University Press.

In India, many people helped me during work on this project; I can single out only a few. In Delhi, I appreciate the invitation of Jyotindra Jain and Kavita Singh to present some of my work at Jawaharlal Nehru University, and the vigorous comments of the faculty and students there. In Mumbai, Rashmi Poddar and Shekhar Bajaj gave me much needed assistance, and in Wardha, I was aided by Bharat Mahodaya and Ashok Mehre. For my visits to Kurukshetra, I am grateful for the help and friendship of Rajendra S. Rana and Anand Pal Tomar. For my time in Pune and Alandi, I thank Sucheta Paranjpe for her assistance.

I have been lucky to have the opportunity to present talks growing out of my work on the biography of the *Gita* at Barnard College, Brown University, Harvard University, Luther College, Tufts University, the University of Michigan, and Yale University. I thank audiences at all of these talks for their stimulating questions.

I am grateful to the National Endowment for the Humanities for a fellowship that enabled me to work full-time on this book, and to Bard College for its support of continuing faculty research. Finally, I wish to acknowledge my gratitude to the students at Bard College over many years who have patiently read through the *Bhagavad Gita* with me and who have engaged in their own dialogues with Krishna.

The *Bhagavad Gita*

Introduction

Dhritarashtra asked: "When my troops and the Pandavas met together, itching for battle, at Kurukshetra, the field of dharma, what happened, Sanjaya?"
—*Bhagavad Gita 1.1*

The *Bhagavad Gita* opens on a field of battle. At Kurukshetra, two massive armies led by the Pandavas and Kauravas have assembled. All the rulers along with the entire warrior class of India are involved, siding with one camp or the other. Leaders blow thunderously on conch shells, while drums and cymbals create a cacophonous roar. Warriors are slapping their arms in eager anticipation. Nearby, packs of jackals and flocks of crows have also assembled, looking forward to a feast of human flesh.

Just as the battle is about to commence, Arjuna, the leading warrior of the Pandava side, asks his charioteer Krishna to station his vehicle in between the two vast forces. "I want to look at the men arrayed here so eager for war," he explains, and Krishna drives his chariot into the no-man's-land. At this moment, Arjuna is overcome with anxiety and despair. He drops his bow and threatens to renounce the battle altogether. It is Krishna's task to persuade Arjuna to overcome his doubts.

The ensuing dialogue between Krishna and Arjuna goes far beyond a rationale for war. It touches on many of the ethical dilemmas, religious practices, and philosophical issues that concerned Indian elites of ancient times. As Krishna instructs Arjuna, he draws on ideas from the many contending schools of thought in classical India, and seeks to integrate them within his own overarching agenda. In the course of their conversation, Krishna reveals to Arjuna that he is the Supreme Lord. Hence this work has long been known by the title *Bhagavad Gita*, the song (*gita*) of the Lord (*bhagavan*).

One can visit the spot in India where this famous dialogue took place. Nowadays a small pilgrimage center, Kurukshetra lies in the fertile plains of Haryana state, in northwestern India, along the course of the dried-up Sarasvati River, once a tributary of the Indus River. In and around the town are numerous sites where significant events in the great battle are supposed to have occurred. At the center of town, overlooking the holy bathing tank used by pilgrims, stands a monumental bronze statue, sixty feet in length and thirty-five feet high, of Krishna and Arjuna in their chariot.

A few miles west of town, the place where Krishna and Arjuna held their conversation is known as "Jyotisar," the essence of illumination. A wide banyan tree, said to be a descendant of an original banyan under which Krishna parked the chariot, marks the exact "Place of the Gita Teaching." Under the shade of the tree now sits a small marble statuette depicting Krishna turning to address Arjuna, protected in a modest marble and glass display case. Also inside the case are two laminated, full-color religious posters and a small booklet of the *Bhagavad Gita* itself. All are adorned with garlands of orange marigolds, white jasmine, and red rose. The tree is surrounded by ponds where one can take a purifying bath, and scattered about the site are several modest shrines dedicated to various Hindu gods and saints. It is a quiet and contemplative place now, like so many former battlefields. When I first journeyed to Jyotisar in January 2010, the only other visitors loitering around the place were young male students from the nearby Institute of Hotel Management.

In India and beyond, one can also celebrate the day on which the *Bhagavad Gita* dialogue happened. The eleventh day of the waxing moon in the lunar month of Margashirsha, which generally falls in December or January, is known as the "Gita Jayanti," the birthday of the *Gita*. Although the age of the *Gita* has been a longstanding matter of uncertainty and debate, the lunar date of the conversation is clearly established in the text. Today the famous conversation is often observed with collective recitations of the seven hundred verses of the *Gita*, accompanied by acts of worship and devotional singing. At Kurukshetra, the locals celebrate Gita Jayanti with particular verve. In addition to recitations and discourses on the *Gita* at the Shri Krishna Museum, the town hosts a five-day Kurukshetra Festival, which includes a procession of musicians and holy men, cultural performances pertaining to the *Gita* in several great tents, political leaders being felicitated, fireworks, and a massive crafts fair of over five hundred displays from throughout India. Beyond India as well, Hindus in Malaysia, Singapore, the United Kingdom, and the United States commemorate the day on which this sacred text was first spoken.

Early in the *Bhagavad Gita*, Krishna tells Arjuna that he has given these same teachings from the beginning of time. And accordingly, many observers have maintained that the dialogue narrated in the *Bhagavad Gita* is not merely a historically specific conversation but in fact an eternal teaching that has universal relevance or an event that takes place at all times. Kurukshetra is both a particular field of battle and perpetual field of *dharma*, or righteousness, as Dhritarashtra's opening question suggests. The medieval Hindu philosopher Shankara (788–820 CE) believed that this dialogue restates the essential teachings of the eternal Vedas. Mohandas Gandhi held that the battlefield of Kurukshetra is located in every human soul, where the perennial conflict between good and evil occurs without end. Devotees of the god Krishna like A. C. Bhaktivedanta, founding teacher of the International Society of Krishna Consciousness, view Krishna to be the Supreme Personality of Godhead, eternally present in the heavenly realm and at the same time recurrently appearing in our world to reenact his timeless activities. The British novelist and essayist Aldous Huxley considered the teachings of Krishna in the *Bhagavad Gita* as the most systematic scriptural statement of a "perennial philosophy" common to all the religions of the world. And countless other readers and reciters over the

FIGURE 1. *Kurukshetra Utsav: Gita Jayanti Samaroh*, poster, unknown artist, 2011.
Author's collection. The poster advertises the 2011 Gita Birthday Festival at Kurukshetra.

centuries have heard in *Gita*'s words something that speaks powerfully to them in their own circumstances.

The doubleness of the *Bhagavad Gita*—its historical specificity and its continuing, even eternal, life—animates this short biography. Whether or not Krishna actually spoke these words to Arjuna under a banyan tree in the Kurukshetra battlefield on the eleventh day of the light fortnight of Margashirsha, the *Bhagavad Gita* was composed at a certain time and place. Most Sanskrit scholars agree that the *Bhagavad Gita* originated in northern India, sometime in the classical period between the reign of the Mauryan king Ashoka (r. 269–232 BCE) and Gupta dynasty (320–547 CE), as part of a much larger poetic composition, the epic poem *Mahabharata*. The dialogue between Krishna and Arjuna, as it has been passed down, was deeply and creatively engaged with the many philosophical and religious currents and disputes of northern Indian during this period. In the course of this discussion, Krishna articulates a complex new religious formulation that encompasses many other existing schools of thought.

Like many great religious works, the *Bhagavad Gita* has outlived its own time and place of composition. The work has lived a vivid and contentious existence over the centuries since, through readings and recitations, translations and commentaries that have reinscribed this classical Indian work into many new currents and disputes. Medieval Brahmin scholars and Krishna devotees, British colonial scholars, German romantics, globe-trotting Hindu gurus, Indian anticolonial freedom fighters, Western students, and spiritual seekers have all engaged in new dialogues with the *Gita*.

My own dialogue with the *Bhagavad Gita* began in the early 1970s, when I was a college student majoring in the history and philosophy of religion. A wave of countercultural fascination with Eastern spirituality had brought the *Gita* to a large, new US audience, and new translations by both scholars and Hindu teachers proliferated. The first version I read was the translation by Bhaktivedanta, Swami Prabhupada, an Indian guru who traveled to the United States in 1965 and established a following of Krishna consciousness. Though intrigued by the work, I was puzzled by its unfamiliar terminology and complicated discussion. Little did I expect that this was the beginning of a lifelong dialogue. A few years later, as a neophyte student of Sanskrit, I tried my hand at reading the *Gita* in its original language. And now, over the past twenty-five years, I have taught the work in college courses on Indian religions, almost as regularly as the Gita Jayanti is celebrated.

Sometime in the nineteenth century, the *Bhagavad Gita* acquired the label of the "Hindu Bible." While the designation is misleading in important respects, since the *Gita* has never enjoyed the canonical authority over the Hindu community that the Hebrew Bible holds for Jews or Christian New Testament has for Christians, it does point to a crucial similarity. Like those more extensive bibles of other traditions, the *Gita* is internally complex and ambiguous enough to have spoken differing truths to different audiences, as suited to their diverse situations and expectations. Like them, it has given rise to two millennia of dialogues, readings, and interpretations. The medieval poet Jnanadeva compared the *Gita* to the legendary multifaceted "wish-granting gem" Chintamani. For centuries new readers have glimpsed the wish-granting *Gita* through its different facets, seeking to bring their own desires toward fulfillment. My book explores those glimpses.

The life of the *Bhagavad Gita* cannot be separated from the identity of its principal speaker, Krishna. Throughout the *Mahabharata*, Krishna appears as a human warrior and ruler, a friend of Arjuna and the other Pandavas, who also has a mysterious other side. For one thing, his upbringing among a tribe of nomadic cowherders is most unusual for a member of the Kshatriya class. More significantly, he reveals his divine nature in the course of the *Gita*. Krishna's own doubleness as a god in human incarnation introduces another layer of complexity to the work. How a reader understands Krishna—as a literary character, historical ruler, wise teacher, incarnate god, or Supreme Lord of All Creation—has crucial bearing also on how one responds to his words in the *Gita*.

The primary aim of this book is to examine the ways that the *Bhagavad Gita* has continued to live through the responses and interpretations of its subsequent readers. This will necessarily be highly selective. The full life of the *Gita* is much too diverse to allow for any comprehensive treatment. The brief seven-hundred-verse poem has been the subject of hundreds of written commentaries in Sanskrit and other Indian languages. It has been translated into more than seventy-five languages worldwide. In English alone, well over three hundred translations of the *Gita* have been published. The *Gita* is a vital text for modern Hindus of many persuasions. Public recitations and oral exegeses are regular events in homes, temples, and auditoriums in India and wherever in the world

Hindus now live. Outside India, the *Gita* is frequently taken as the first and most representative work for those first seeking to understand Hinduism. It appears regularly as a primary reading in hundreds of college courses on Hinduism and Asian religions throughout North America and elsewhere.

To gain some purchase on the sprawling life of this text, we will look at the broader devotional cult surrounding the divine character of Krishna, and briefly examine some of the ways medieval Indian commentators emphasized different core "disciplines" (*yoga*) and different ontological positions articulated within the *Gita*. We will trace how the *Gita* traveled from India to the West, through translations into English and other European languages, and how it was appropriated into new areas of concern. We will explore how Indian nationalists utilized the poem in their struggle against colonial control—a new Kurukshetra battlefield, as they saw it—and how they debated the *Gita's* fundamental directives. And we will look at a few of the ways contemporary translators and teachers reanimate the classical poem for modern audiences in India and beyond. First, though, it will be valuable to situate the *Bhagavad Gita* in its own original context: its compositional birthday.

The *Bhagavad Gita* in the Time of Its Composition

"Oh, what a great crime we are about to commit! From our desire to enjoy kingship, we are ready to kill our own kinsmen. It would be better for me if Dhritarashtra's sons with their weapons in hand were to kill me in combat, unarmed and unresisting." And after he said this, Arjuna, with a grief-stricken heart, threw aside his bow and arrows and sat down in the back of his chariot.

—*Bhagavad Gita 1.45–47*

The *Bhagavad Gita* forms part of the *Mahabharata*, a vast epic poem in classical Sanskrit that tells the story of a devastating rivalry between two clans of the ruling class for control of a kingdom in northern India. The *Gita* consists of a dialogue between two leading characters in this epic, Arjuna and Krishna, at a tense moment just as war between the two sides is about to begin. The conversation deals with the moral propriety of the war and much else as well. The *Gita* begins with Arjuna in confusion and despair, dropping his weapons; it ends with Arjuna picking up his bow, all doubts resolved and ready for battle. Once he does so, the war begins, and the narrative of the *Mahabharata* continues.

From an early date, the *Bhagavad Gita* also circulated as an independent work. It has been read, recited, interpreted, commented on, transcribed, translated, and published as a self-standing work of religious philosophy. This double identity of the *Gita*, as both a portion of a larger epic story and autonomous text, is an important source of its power and appeal. In this biographical account of the *Bhagavad Gita*, primary attention will be given to the life of the *Gita* on its own. But to gain a full sense of the rhetorical power that this text had in its own time of composition, it is also necessary to consider the *Gita* in its larger epic context.

The *Gita* in the *Mahabharata*

In the *Mahabharata* two sets of brothers, related as cousins to one another, vie for the throne of Hastinapura, capital of northern India.[1] The five Pandava brothers are the sons of Pandu and his two wives; the hundred Kaurava brothers are the offspring of Dhritarashtra, elder brother to Pandu. The kingdom is beset with problems of dynastic continuity of a convoluted nature, going back several generations. Dhritarashtra is born blind, ordinarily a disqualification for kingship in classical India, and so the younger Pandu initially rules. When Pandu dies as a result of imprecated lovemaking with his younger wife, Dhritarashtra assumes the throne and takes in the orphaned sons of his brother. The Pandavas and Kauravas grow up together in Hastinapura. As they are educated and trained together as members of the Kshatriya or warrior class, a deep rivalry grows between the two groups. Uncertainty looms as to who will succeed Dhritarashtra. Duryodhana, the eldest of the Kauravas, is particularly adamant in his efforts to disinherit and destroy his cousins, the Pandavas.

Faced with unremitting antagonism between the cousins, the elders decide to partition the kingdom—an unwelcome necessity. The Pandavas are sent out to the hinterlands, where they set up court in a new capital, Indraprastha, along the Yamuna River where Delhi now stands. Their success in building up their new kingdom virtually from scratch only exacerbates the jealousy of Duryodhana and the other Kauravas. After a series of confrontations, culminating in a dice game with the highest possible stakes, the Pandavas are finally forced into a fourteen-year exile. Eventually, though, they return to seek what they see as rightfully theirs. Animosity grows ever greater, and reconciliation becomes impossible. As war appears increasingly inevitable, both sides round up allies until the entire ruling class of India is involved on one side or the other. The two camps proceed to the northern plains of Kurukshetra, agree to rules of combat, and line up facing one another. It is at this moment that the warrior Arjuna asks his charioteer Krishna to drive their vehicle into the no-man's-land between the two sides so he can survey the enemy combatants.

Arjuna is the third of the five Pandava brothers, and most skilled warrior among them. When growing up at Hastinapura, Arjuna is the one who prevails in the contests that their teacher Drona holds for the Pandavas and

Kauravas. While the Pandavas are in exile, Arjuna goes on a lengthy quest for weapons in anticipation of the conflict to come. He performs extraordinary austerities, wrestles with the god Shiva, lives for awhile in the heaven of the god Indra, and returns with the most awesome divine weaponry in the world. Now with the battle about to begin, Arjuna is the powerful Pandava warrior that the Kaurava side most fears.

In the *Mahabharata*, Arjuna's chariot driver Krishna appears as the ruler of a kingdom in western India. He meets the Pandavas when they are in hiding and quickly forms a special friendship with them. One of Pandu's wives, Kunti, is sister to Krishna's father, so they are already related as cousins. Later Krishna persuades Arjuna to abduct and marry his sister Subhadra, thereby tightening the relationship between them as brothers-in-law. Krishna acts as adviser to the Pandavas and also diplomat, unsuccessfully seeking reconciliation between the two camps just before the battle. But there is another side to Krishna, which becomes apparent from time to time. He is also divine. His godly status is not generally visible to other characters within the epic narrative, and is recognized only by a few unusually wise or fortunate figures. In the *Bhagavad Gita*, as we will see, Krishna powerfully reveals the full extent of his divine nature to Arjuna.

Shortly before the battle, both Duryodhana and Arjuna travel to visit Krishna in his palace. Each wishes to enlist Krishna's aid for his own side in the war. To avoid favoritism, Krishna offers them a choice. One may have

Krishna's enormous army of a million trained warriors; the other may have Krishna himself, but only as a weaponless noncombatant. Duryodhana chooses troops, and Arjuna requests Krishna's personal assistance. Both Duryodhana and Arjuna are happy with the outcome. Duryodhana believes that Krishna's myriad troops will assure a Kaurava victory. Arjuna asks that Krishna serve in the humble position of a charioteer, a role not usually taken by a member of the warrior class. As Arjuna's chariot driver, Krishna will remain in close proximity during the battle to advise and counsel his friend, cousin, and brother-in-law Arjuna.

When the battle lines have formed at Kurukshetra, Arjuna and Krishna look over the two sides. Drums are pounding, conches blasting, cymbals ringing—all creating a terrifying roar. Suddenly Arjuna loses all his zeal for battle. He sees his own cousins, grandfathers, uncles, in-laws, and teachers in the opposing Kaurava army. Surely it is not worthy to fight and kill one's own kin. Arjuna is overcome with grief and indecision. His entire body trembles, his mind whirls in confusion, and he drops his fearsome bow. "I will not fight," he declares (*Bhagavad Gita* 2.9).[2]

For Krishna this is a crisis. If the Pandavas are to have any chance of victory in the upcoming battle, they will need their most powerful warrior to be fully committed. The charioteer recognizes that his first task is to convince Arjuna to overcome all his anxieties and uncertainties. Krishna's counseling session forms the conversation recounted in the *Bhagavad Gita*.

This dialogue of roughly seven hundred verses requires about an hour and a half to recite. Some observers have pointed to the unlikelihood, or the "dramatic absurdity," as one noted Indologist put it, of great masses of zealous warriors sitting idly by for ninety minutes while a soldier and his charioteer chat in the no-man's-land. Yet verisimilitude is not the aim of the epic here. This is a pause in the narrative action, a *sandhi* or "juncture" in the story, as classical Indian rhetoric would label it. Here two central characters in the *Mahabharata* reflect once again on the morality of the war along with the ultimate religious issues that such life-and-death struggles so often raise.

Krishna's Battlefield Teachings

Though his body is shaking and his mind is spinning, Arjuna is able to articulate to Krishna the main causes of his distress. One is psychological. He feels deep pity and grief over the deaths sure to ensue during the battle. He sees no possible good that could compensate for the terrible losses from a war involving kin. The other is moral. Arjuna is confused as to his duty (dharma) in this situation. On the one hand, his responsibility as a member of the warrior class is to engage in appropriate battle. On the other hand, he owes a duty of protection to his own family members. When family obligations are not observed, Arjuna argues, the entire social order collapses. The opposite side in this battle is filled with Arjuna's relatives. So

Krishna's efforts at persuasion must start with these two issues.

"The truly learned person," the charioteer begins, "does not grieve over those who are dead and those not dead" (2.11). The dead do not cease to exist. Krishna's assertion here rests on the premise of transmigration or metempsychosis: that a person's essential spirit or soul existed already before birth, and will continue to exist after death. Just as a person might take off one set of clothes and put on a new one, so too at death the person's soul dispenses with one used body and enters into a fresh new one. This is nothing new. Krishna is correct in observing that most of the "truly learned" schools of thought in classical India had come to accept the theory of transmigration in some form or another. The challenging part for Arjuna is to apply this radical redefinition of death to the situation of war. If only the body dies, then killing other soldiers in battle really only extinguishes those soldiers' bodies, leaving their soul to move on to other ones. If Arjuna can fully accept this philosophical perspective, Krishna tells him, then he has no reason to grieve over war casualties.

As for Arjuna's dilemma over conflicting duties, Krishna responds succinctly. Your duty as a member of the warrior class, to fight in a righteous battle, the charioteer asserts, trumps any obligations you may feel toward other members of your family (2.31). As the treatises on dharma state, it is part of the inherent nature of males of the Kshatriya class to engage in war. Krishna returns to this notion near the end of his address to Arjuna.

"It is better to do your own duty, even poorly, than to perform the duty of someone else well" (18.47). Arjuna must follow his own nature as well as his class duty, and in doing so he will not commit any fault.

Thus Krishna responds to the two explicit causes of Arjuna's distress. The conversation could have ended there. But Arjuna gives no indication that he is convinced yet, and Krishna is just getting started. At this point, still early in their dialogue, Krishna proposes to explain a method that can "cut away the bondage of action" (2.39).

What does Krishna mean by "bondage of action"? He refers here to some of the prevalent theories of action in classical India. Religious philosophers of various schools (Buddhist and Jain as well as Hindu) identified desire, the primary motivation for action, to be a fundamental problem. Undertaking an act out of desire, they maintained, leads to bondage. The key term here is *karma*, which in its primary usage simply denotes action. In classical India, however, karma also had come to refer to the persisting moral consequences of actions. (It is in this extended sense that the term has been incorporated into the modern English lexicon.) Many envisioned karma as a residue that adhered to a person's self or soul, like some kind of opaque grime that obscured its intrinsic clarity. This buildup of karma caused a soul to be reborn again and again in bondage to the world of suffering. The way to avoid this bondage, therefore, was to avoid all desire-based action. And to accomplish this, it was necessary to leave behind one's familial and social responsibilities, and become a renouncer. As a homeless mendicant, one could avoid acting out of desire, practice disciplines of meditation and austerity, and seek a state of liberation from all bondage—a state that transcended human suffering. Hindus most often called it *moksha*, Buddhists termed it *nirvana*, and Jains designated it *kaivalya*, but all the advocates of renunciation viewed it as the highest state.

Why should Krishna bring this up here, on the battlefield? Arjuna is no Buddhist monk or Jain ascetic, yet he is proposing to renounce an action that is his social responsibility. Krishna is urging Arjuna to engage in violent battle, an especially gruesome form of action. There were examples in classical India of rulers who did renounce their war making in favor of higher ethical values, such as the famous Buddhist emperor Ashoka Maurya (r. 270–230 BCE). So Krishna feels that he must reconcile his advocacy of worldly action with the religious claims of the renunciatory schools. To do so, he proposes a new theory of action.

One can act without being driven by desire, says Krishna. The key is to avoid any attachment to the results (or fruits) of your action.

> Your obligation is to the action, and never to its fruits. Do not be motivated by the fruit of your actions. But do not become attached to non-action, either. Abandon your attachment and engage in worldly action, Arjuna, while standing firm in discipline (*yoga*). Consider success and failure to be equal. This equanimity is called discipline, Arjuna, since the action itself is much less important than the discipline of the intellect. (2.47–49)

This is one of the primary arguments of the *Bhagavad Gita*. One need not, and in fact should not, avoid worldly action. To avoid the bondage that results from actions driven by desires, however, one must avoid any attachment to the ends or fruits of that action. One must maintain a mental equanimity toward the outcome. This requires a firm disciplining of the mind. Arjuna should fight in the war, as it is his class duty to do so, and if he does this without any concern for success or failure, without desire for any fruits of victory or fear of defeat, no "bondage of action" will attach to him. This leaves open the path to liberation. "Through discipline of the intellect," Krishna adds, "wise people renounce the fruits born of action, and freed from the bondage that leads to rebirth, they go to the unblemished state" (2.51).

With this new theory of action, Krishna has provided a way for Arjuna to engage in the upcoming battle without incurring the bondage that normally results from desire-based action. As Arjuna immediately recognizes, though, this theory is easier said than done. How does one gain the kind of mental equilibrium that would enable acting without any attachment to the fruits of that action? Arjuna imagines it can only be an extraordinary person, one whose "wisdom is firm" (*sthitaprajna*), and so he asks Krishna for a description of such a person (2.54).

To gain this sort of mastery over the self, one must employ discipline. The term here is yoga, the Indic word that has come to enjoy a complex and expansive life in modern global culture. In classical India, itinerant seekers and organized groups of renouncers had experimented with a wide range of disciplinary practices directed at the body and mind—fasting and abstinences, physical postures, breath control, sensory withdrawal, mental concentration, and the like. Here Krishna suggests that these disciplines can be adapted by those who are not renouncers, those still active in worldly affairs, to gain the self-mastery required for detached action. To become a person whose wisdom is firm, one must first gain control over the senses. As the winds of a tempest carry away a ship at sea, so the senses can draw the self into all sorts of unwanted attachments. Better, says Krishna, to learn to withdraw the senses from their objects, as a turtle draws its limbs back into its firm shell. For when one can remain serene, without any attraction or repulsion toward the objects of the world, that equanimity can lead to liberation (2.55–71).

Krishna's description of the person of firm wisdom, the sthitaprajna, raises a new question for Arjuna. If that is the goal, what is the best way to reach such a state? Arjuna's concern here reflects the broader religious situation in classical India. There were numerous schools of religious and philosophical thought all advancing their own claims as to the surest method to attain the best goal. How was one to decide which path to follow? "Tell me for certain," Arjuna implores Krishna, "the one means by which I can gain the highest end" (3.2).

In the course of the following dialogue, Krishna discusses many of these methods of spiritual attainment. Later commentators have conveniently classified them into three overarching means or "paths" (*marga*): the discipline of action (*karma yoga*), discipline of knowledge (*jnana yoga*), and discipline of devotion (*bhakti yoga*). As we will see, later interpreters have frequently selected one or another of these paths as the most important or effective. Krishna praises all of them as worthy. He also evaluates the efficacy of each in terms of his own theory of action. That is, he judges disciplines most effective insofar as they are grounded in a mental state of equanimity or detachment from the fruits of action, or lead to such a state.

Krishna discusses the path of action most often in relation to the Vedic practice of sacrifice (*yajna*). Orthodox Brahmins considered this the preeminent form of religious action, leading to all kinds of benefits. Those most loyal to the Vedic practices believe the sacrificial actions to be automatically efficacious. As Krishna reframes it, by contrast, the crucial issue is not the action itself but rather the mentality with which the action is performed. "When one performs sacrifice without attachment, freely, his mind held firm through proper knowledge, his *karma* disappears completely" (4.23). Sacrifices that are undertaken with a desire to attain some fruit, whether that be success or enjoyments in this world or the next, will lead to the bondage of action; they will bind the person to future rebirths. But sacrificial actions of any sort that are performed with true mental equanimity, with detachment from the fruits of action, will lead to superior spiritual ends. The same holds true for Arjuna on the battlefield. He should engage in battle as his duty, without any attachment to the outcome, as a kind of sacrificial act.

As for the discipline of knowledge, Krishna surveys several different philosophical systems that aim to present full analyses of the underlying structure of the world. Proper knowledge of this structure, they assume, has a liberating power. The most important of these systems for Krishna's discussion are early forms of the schools known as Samkhya (enumeration) and Vedanta (culmination of the Veda). Krishna grants qualified approval to these ways of analyzing or understanding the world. The Samkhya system divided reality into a fundamental dualism of the Soul (*purusha*) and Substance (*prakriti*). If one truly understands that the observing Soul stands separately from the categories of Substance, one can avoid attachment even in the midst of action. Because this analysis can lead to detachment, Krishna judges it to be valuable. Drawing on the speculations and insights of the Upanishads, the emerging Vedanta school of classical India developed a monistic analysis of reality, in which the eternal Soul (*atman*) was said to be one with an unchanging Absolute, termed *brahman*. All else is said to be ephemeral. In Krishna's view, this way of comprehending the world could equally lead to firm wisdom in action. The philosophical criterion Krishna employs in his discussion of these schools of knowledge is not their metaphysical accuracy but rather the psychological consequences for one who adopts that perspective. He grants each a heuristic validity insofar as it leads one toward equanimity, but he does not endorse a single unitary system. Krishna is after a larger unity.

While the paths of action and knowledge draw on familiar religious practices or schools of thought, the path of devotion is something new within Sanskrit literature.

In religious usage the term *bhakti*, translated as devotion, denotes a vital living relationship between a human devotee and a god. The *Bhagavad Gita* provides the earliest treatment in Indic literature of a religious orientation that would be of enormous significance for the subsequent development of Hinduism and other Indian religious traditions as well. Krishna places this disciplinary newcomer on an equal footing with the other disciplines, and even at times elevates it above them.

The path of devotion involves strict discipline, just as the others do. One must cultivate an attitude of loyalty and adoration, a willingness to carry out the service of god. As with the other paths, this involves a subordination of the ego, an elimination of self-interest. But devotion also requires a worthy target or recipient of that devotion. In the course of their discussion on the battlefield, Krishna gradually reveals himself to Arjuna as exactly that worthy recipient: not just any old god, but the Supreme Deity of them all. Krishna's presentation of the way of devotion and his divine self-revelation go hand in hand.

Early on in their dialogue, Krishna tells Arjuna that he has given these same teachings long ago to the Sun, who taught it to the first man and then to the first king of the solar dynasty (4.1). Arjuna is understandably perplexed, since he regards Krishna as his human friend, about the same age as he is. How could he possibly have conveyed these same teachings to such ancient figures? Krishna reiterates the notion of reincarnation, which implies that both of them have lived many previous lives, but then adds something new. Unlike Arjuna, he has taken on his birth knowingly and intentionally. "I have gone through many births, and so have you," Krishna explains to Arjuna. "But I know them all, and you do not. Even though I am unborn, and even though I am the imperishable Lord of all Beings, I take birth by entering into my own physical form, by my own supernal power" (4.5–6). Further, he states, he has come with a purpose. "For whenever there is a decline in righteousness (*dharma*) and an increase in un-righteousness, Arjuna, then I emanate myself. For the pro-tection of good people, for the destruction of evil-doers, and for the restoration of righteousness, I take birth in age after age" (4.7–8). Here in its first explicit appearance is the concept of Krishna's (or Vishnu's) *avatara*: his incar-nation, or more literally "crossing down" into human or other physical form. (And here is another classical Indic term that has reincarnated itself firmly in modern English usage and global culture—in this case, through computer role-playing games and a Hollywood blockbuster.) In this brief exchange Krishna reveals two key elements in his own theology. He is a transcendent deity (the "Lord of All Beings") who also takes on material forms (such as his cur-rent embodiment as Krishna), and he does so in order to intervene in worldly affairs and support righteousness.

Krishna goes on to elaborate this divine self-portrait in great detail. He encompasses all the other gods. He is the unborn, unchanging, undying, unmanifest, all creat-ing, the source, the atman, the brahman, the One. In short, he lays claim to all the terms that philosophers in classical India had employed to point to the Absolute. But in contrast to the Absolute that the Upanishads had characterized in largely apophatic terms, Krishna the new Absolute simultaneously has a more immediate, palpable, visible identity. There he stands, in apparently mortal human form, in the front of Arjuna's chariot. The theology of the *Gita* requires this double recognition: Krishna is the Supreme Being who is both transcendent and physically present. The later Vaishnava philosopher Ramanuja (1017–1137 CE) describes this seeming paradox as the co-existent "supremacy" (*paratva*) and "easy accessibility" (*saulabhya*) of the Lord.

Krishna's revelation has fundamental implications for all three paths. If it is the case that Krishna is truly the Highest Lord, then it makes sense to direct all sacrifices to him. Moreover, if he is truly ubiquitous, he is already present in all the elements of the sacrificial rituals. "I am the rite," he tells Arjuna, "I am the sacrifice, I am the offering, I am the herb, I am the mantra, I am the ghee, I am the fire, I am the oblation" (9.16). The ritual of sacrifice becomes a series of activities within the totality that is Krishna.

The path of knowledge, likewise, involves the recognition of Krishna as the best part or inner essence of all things. "In water I am the taste," Krishna proclaims. "I am the light in the sun and the moon. In all the Vedas I am OM, in the ether sound, and in men their virility. I am the good smell in the earth and the fiery energy in the sun. In every living being I am the life force, and in ascetics I am their ascetic power. Know me, Arjuna, as the eternal seed of all things, the wisdom of the wise, and the charisma of those who shine" (7.8–10). Yet knowledge may have its limitations, too. There is something fundamentally paradoxical about this immanent Absolute, and Krishna seems to take pleasure in placing himself just beyond Arjuna's conceptual reach.

> This entire world is stretched out from me, in my unmanifest form. All creatures reside within me, but I do not reside in them. And yet again, all creatures do not reside within me. Behold my lordly yoga! I support all creatures and bring them into existence, but my self does not reside in them. Just as the great wind goes everywhere and yet remains within space, so all beings reside within me. Think about that! (9.4–6)

Even the gods are unable to know Krishna's full extent, since he is the one and only Original God.

The discipline of devotion can involve both action and knowledge. Any act, no matter how modest, can become an act of devotion. Once again, it is not the action that counts but the mentality of the actor instead. "If one presents to me a leaf, a flower, a fruit, or water, with devotion," Krishna explains, "I accept that offering of devotion from the donor. Therefore, Arjuna, whenever you act, make an offering, sacrifice, donate something, or undertake an ascetic practice, do so as an offering to me, and you will be freed from the bondage of your action, whether good or bad results" (9. 27–28). Devotion is a new way of cutting away the bondage of any act. One can abandon all personal attachment to the fruits by redirecting that action into a devotional service toward Krishna. Similarly, holding on to the perception of Krishna as all pervasive can lead from knowledge to devotion. "If a person sees me in everything, and sees everything in me," Krishna tells Arjuna, "I will not disappear from that person, nor will that one disappear from me" (6.30). This understanding, he continues, will lead a person to an immersion in Krishna's very being: "However he moves, he moves in me" (6.31).

Thus devotion becomes a discipline that is not simply one among several paths but rather enters into and transforms other disciplines. By this standard Krishna judges the person who practices the discipline of devotion as superior to others.

> I consider that *yogin* [the one who practices bhakti yoga] to be superior to ascetics. He is superior to those who practice the discipline of knowledge and he is superior to those who practice the discipline of action. Therefore, Arjuna, be that kind of *yogin*. I consider the one who faithfully shares in me, and whose innermost self is absorbed in me, to be the most disciplined of all *yogins*. (6.46–47)

Additionally, he emphasizes, this path is open to all: "Those who take refuge in Me, even women, Vaishyas, Shudras, or those born impure, they nevertheless reach the highest destination" (9.32). For Arjuna, faced with the daunting prospect of war, devotion offers a new way of grounding his own actions. This is exactly what Krishna recommends. "Finding yourself in this impermanent and unhappy world, join yourself to me," he concludes. "Fix your mind on me, devote yourself to me, sacrifice to me, honor me, and with your self yoked to me as its highest end, you will come to me" (9.33–34).

At this point Arjuna is fully convinced of Krishna's divine nature. Still, he would like one further bit of evidence. So far Krishna has stood in front of him in the chariot, a human being explaining in words his own divine nature. Now Arjuna wishes to see Krishna's "lordly form." Krishna complies. First, though, he must grant Arjuna "divine vision." Krishna himself does not change, but the transformation in Arjuna's capacity to see enables the warrior to see what is already present. And what a reality he sees!

Initially, Arjuna perceives a visual confirmation of what Krishna has already explained verbally. Arjuna sees Krishna's arms and eyes, bellies and mouths, stretching out in all directions. He views all the gods contained within Krishna's vast body. Krishna fills the entire space of the world. It is an awesome sight, but as the vision unfolds, Arjuna becomes increasingly alarmed. "I quake in my innermost being," he pleads, "and I cannot find firm ground or peace" (11.24). The Supreme Deity is turning into a world-destroying fire. Arjuna begins to see a distorted premonition of the battle to come, with Krishna at its destructive vortex.

> All the sons of Dhritarashtra along with the legions of kings who rule the earth, Bhishma, Drona, that charioteer's son Karna, and the leaders of our armies too, are all rushing into your fearsome mouths gaping with fangs. I see some dangling between your teeth

with their heads already crushed. Like a multitude of gushing torrents of rivers rushing headlong to the ocean, these heroes of the human world are flooding into your flaming mouths. As swiftly as moths fly into a blazing fire to die, just as quickly these men are entering mouths to die. (11.26–29)

This is a long way from the friend and charioteer Krishna, and from the benign dharma-supporting incarnation Krishna. In confusion, Arjuna asks just who this terrifying being is. "I am Time," replies this supernal form of Krishna, "powerful destroyer of worlds, grown immense here to annihilate these men" (11.32).

This is the other side of Krishna's absoluteness. If he is the agent of all creation, he is also god of destruction. The upcoming battle appears to be a gigantic act of disintegration, carried out ultimately by Krishna acting as Time. This places Arjuna's role in the war in still another new light. If God is the true agent of this all-consuming war, then the responsibility of Arjuna or any other warrior in it changes. Krishna clarifies this for Arjuna: "Therefore, rise up and gain fame," he commands. "Conquer your enemies and rule a prosperous kingdom. They have already been destroyed by me. You will be my mere instrument, Arjuna. Drona, Bhishma, Jayadratha, Karna, and still other battle heroes are slain by me. You kill them" (11.33–34). As a devotee of Krishna, Arjuna should now carry out his duty as a warrior, with the understanding that his actions serve as an instrument of the divine will.

FIGURE 2. *Sampurna Viratsvarup* (Krishna in his supernal form),
chromolithograph by B. G. Sharma, ca. 1965.
Published by Sharma Picture Publications. Author's collection.

This is all a bit much for Arjuna. He falls down before this Supreme Lord and asks to see Krishna "just as you were before" (11.46). Perhaps it is not humanly possible to sustain such visionary insight, or perhaps Arjuna's new perspective on the war is overwhelming. Krishna generously removes the divine vision, and Arjuna recovers his wits when he sees just his human friend Krishna easily accessible in the chariot with him.

Part of the larger narrative of the *Mahabharata*, the *Bhagavad Gita* is itself a narrative. Opening with a warrior's crisis of grief and indecision, it proceeds through a rising action of teachings, as Krishna guides Arjuna through issues of morality, soteriology, and theology. With Arjuna's acceptance of this new perspective, Krishna concludes by granting his listener an overpowering but temporary visual insight into his own all-encompassing nature. (Later texts refer to this as the *Vishvarupa*, the "All Form.") The *Gita* narrative might have ended with this, but it does not. As a new devotee Arjuna still requires further instruction, and so immediately after recovering from his state of panic he asks Krishna, "Who are the better *yogins*?" (12.1). Krishna promptly answers, and so the battlefield dialogue continues, in a lengthy denouement. These later discussions are best seen as amplifications, corollaries, and extensions of the main points Krishna has already conveyed.

At the end of the *Bhagavad Gita*, however, Krishna suggests one final wrinkle in the fabric of his teachings. He calls it the "biggest mystery of them all."

Think about this knowledge I have taught you fully, the most secret of secrets, and then you can do as you wish. But first, listen to one last utterance of mine, the biggest mystery of them all. Since I love you very much, I will tell you this for your benefit. Hold me in your heart, be my devotee, sacrifice to me, honor me, and you will surely come to me. I promise you this, for you are loved by me. Abandon all your duties and take refuge with me alone. I will liberate you from all sins. Do not grieve. (18.62–66)

Some later schools of Hinduism have considered this the culminating or ultimate teaching of the entire *Gita*. First Krishna states his love for Arjuna. Up to now, the concept of bhakti has focused on the loyalty and love of the devotee toward God, but here God returns the love. There is emotional reciprocity in bhakti. Moreover, if one is fully devoted to God, even moral duties may be abandoned. After strongly supporting duty as the foundation for detached or selfless action throughout his earlier teachings, Krishna seems to allow an antinomian escape clause for the true devotee who takes refuge in God alone. In the end, Krishna takes responsibility for granting liberation to Arjuna, or to anyone completely devoted to him.

"So, is all your ignorant delusion destroyed?" Krishna asks. Arjuna answers that he has overcome all his initial doubts and is prepared to follow Krishna's directives. He is ready now to fight in the great war to come.

The Fruits of War

If Krishna's teachings in the *Bhagavad Gita* provide a persuasive rationale for Arjuna to fight, the *Mahabharata* does not shy away from the dire consequences of that decision. Many readers have seen the *Gita* as articulating the essential moral, ideological, or theological message of the *Mahabharata* as a whole. If so, it is a bracing message indeed. The *Mahabharata* offers a grim story of consuming war suffused with loss and grief.

Once Arjuna accedes to Krishna's argument and picks up his bow, the soldiers massed on the great field of the Kurus roar in anticipation and excitement. Even the gods gather to watch. The fight is on in earnest, and Arjuna will participate in it with all his energy and ability. It will last for eighteen days, and the scale of death will be overwhelming.

At the onset, both sides have agreed to the rules of engagement. As the battle wears on, however, these ethical guidelines for battle fall by the wayside and the warriors become immersed in spiraling cycles of increasingly brutal vengeance. Often it is Krishna who urges the Pandavas to employ low blows and lies to defeat their enemies, and frequently Arjuna is the one who dutifully follows his guidance. The carnage is tremendous on both sides. By the end, nearly the entire warrior class of India has been exterminated. Kurukshetra is covered with the corpses of men, horses, and elephants. Yudhishthira, the eldest Pandava brother, calculates at the conclusion that 1,660,020,000 men have been slain. Only a few Kshatriya males survive, including the five Pandava brothers, Krishna, and a handful of others. The Kshatriya women, meanwhile, wail and moan as they stream on to the battlefield, chasing away the jackals and crows as they search for the butchered remains of their husbands, sons, brothers, and fathers.

In the aftermath of this cataclysm, the victorious Pandavas are responsible for restoring sovereign rule. As the eldest son of Pandu, it falls to Yudhishthira to claim the throne. He is so filled with grief over what has transpired and his own feelings of culpability that he stubbornly resists. In our modern clinical vocabulary, he suffers from posttraumatic stress disorder. Only after the lengthy urging of Krishna and others does Yudhishthira agree reluctantly to take up his Kshatriya duty and be consecrated as king. Yudhishthira later performs a horse sacrifice that validates his uncontested imperial overlordship on the subcontinent. At the conclusion of the epic, after thirty-two years of sovereignty, Yudhishthira and his brothers retire from the capital and head north into the Himalayas in hopes of reaching heaven.

How does one comprehend a holocaust of such magnitude? Yudhishthira, Arjuna, and the other survivors within the story struggle for the rest of their lives to swallow the bitter fruits of the war. Their grief never ends, though they do manage to carry on their responsibilities in the postwar world.

The *Mahabharata* itself provides several broad frames for understanding the war at the center of the epic. One is sacrifice. In line with Vedic tradition, sacrifice is central to the maintenance of order at every level, both human and cosmic. In the situation of extreme disorder in the warrior class described at the epic's beginning, only an extreme form of sacrifice can restore order within human society. The *Mahabharata* thus traces a narrative arc from a corrupt and fractious ruling class with multiple contentious centers of power, through an all-consuming war that is seen as a comprehensive human sacrifice, to the establishment of a unitary Indian Empire presided over by the just king Yudhishthira.

A second frame projects this eschatological interpretation in cosmic terms. The *Mahabharata* relates a cosmic purging. The Earth herself is overrun by demons, who have taken on human form as Kshatriyas, and requires an apocalyptic battle to rid herself of this malign force and reestablish earthly order. In terms of Indian notions of cyclic time, a great universal dissolution can then be followed by a new creation. This broad vision validates Krishna's incarnation as a salvific figure and Arjuna's vision of Krishna's role in the battle, revealed in the *Bhagavad Gita*, as prime mover in this necessary revolving of the wheel of time.

Following these textual leads, later Indian tradition has often identified the transformative events described in the *Mahabharata* as marking the transition from one era to another. The war at Kurukshetra, it is said, represents the final deterioration of the Dvapara era, and the subsequent establishment of orderly rule begins a new era, the Kali-yuga, the one in which we now live. The *Mahabharata* therefore documents the founding events of the present.

Composition

Who composed the *Bhagavad Gita*? One may respond to this question in several ways.

One answer is that God did it. That is, Krishna, who reveals himself in the course of his discourse to be the incarnate Supreme Deity, conveyed these teachings to Arjuna, much as he had in the distant past and will continue to do in the future. The *Gita* itself endorses this perspective, and many Hindu believers through the centuries have readily accepted divine authorship. But textual historians are not generally satisfied with attributions of divine authorship to religious scriptures. We prefer human authors, and preferably humans with names, dates, and places. Some have tried to identify a human historical Krishna, as we will see, although the evidence for this is scanty.

The most common traditional Indian answer does supply a name. Vyasa is the author of the *Mahabharata* and hence of the *Bhagavad Gita* within it. He is a Brahmin sage who appears as a character within the *Mahabharata*. In fact, Vyasa plays quite a seminal role in the story, since he is the genetic grandfather to both the Pandava and Kaurava fraternities. When the ruling king of the Bharata dynasty, Vichitravirya, dies without fathering a male heir, Vyasa (who is a half brother to the deceased) is called to court in order to impregnate his two widows. Their sons are Pandu and Dhritarashtra, fathers of the Pandavas and Kauravas, respectively. Vyasa remains offstage during much of the *Mahabharata* story, happily meditating in his ashram. From time to time, however, he is called into action and intervenes vigorously in the narrative attributed to him. Thus Vyasa is, as the rhetorical critics would say, a "dramatized narrator" involved in his own tale. Textual historians generally prefer terms that undercut any implication of Vyasa's actual authorship. They refer to Vyasa as a "mythical" or "symbolic" author of the *Mahabharata*.[3]

The *Mahabharata* itself supplies a more complex answer to the question of authorship. The name Vyasa means divider, compiler, and diffuser. Vyasa is famous for "dividing" the unitary Veda into four Vedas, according to tradition. Within the *Mahabharata*, he appears as one link in a chain of authorship, a compiler whose compilation is in turn retold, supplemented, and diffused by others.

The dialogue of Krishna and Arjuna on the battlefield of Kurukshetra that constitutes the *Bhagavad Gita* is observed by Sanjaya, an attendant at the Hastinapura court. Vyasa has granted divine vision to Sanjaya for the duration of the war, and this special gift enables Sanjaya to hear the *Gita* dialogue even without accompanying the pair on to the battlefield. Through this divine ability, he temporarily becomes an omniscient narrator. Sanjaya dutifully reports this conversation and the entire battle (covering five books, or nearly one-third of the entire epic) to the blind king Dhritarashtra, father of the Kauravas, seated in the royal palace at Hastinapura, over a hundred miles from Kurukshetra. Subsequently the Brahmin sage Vyasa assembles Sanjaya's account, other lengthy portions spoken by others, and his own connective narration into a single epic composition. Thus he is, as his name suggests, the compiler in the *Mahabharata*. At his ashram, he teaches this great poem to five Brahmin pupils.

Long after the war at Kurukshetra, Arjuna's great-grandson, Janamejaya, performs a large snake sacrifice at Taxila. The long-lived Vyasa attends the sacrifice together with his disciples. Since Vyasa has been an eyewitness to the deeds of the Pandavas and Kauravas, Janamejaya asks him to tell the story of his lineage's ancestral battle. Vyasa directs his pupil Vaishampayana to relate the tale just as he has heard it. Vaishampayana obediently recites the epic story he has learned from his teacher to the king. Most of the *Mahabharata* consists of the conversation between Vaishampayana and Janamejaya. Yet this is not the end of it.

One of the attentive auditors at Taxila is Ugrashravas, an itinerant bard. After listening to the full narration of Vaishampayana, Ugrashravas travels to an ashram in Nai-misha Forest, where he meets Shaunaka and a group of Brahmin sages who are engaged in a lengthy twelve-year sacrifice. With much time on their hands, the sages ask Ugrashravas about Janamejaya's snake sacrifice and the great story that Vaishampayana has recited there. Ugrashravas retells the story and supplements it with ad-ditional materials. Finally, there is one last frame in the Russian matryoshka-like structure of oral narrations: the anonymous narrator who relates to us, the outermost au-dience, the scene at the Naimisha ashram encompassing Ugrashravas's version of Vaishampayana's recitation of Vyasa's compilation containing Sanjaya's account of the conversation between Krishna and Arjuna on the

Kurukshetra battlefield The *Mahabharata* thus portrays its own composition as a complex sequence of oral retellings involving multiple speakers.

Indological scholars in India and the West have long debated the question of the historical composition of the *Mahabharata* and *Bhagavad Gita*. For a work as vast, intricate, and diffuse as the *Mahabharata*, few textual historians have accepted a historical Vyasa as a "single genius." Most assume some form of multiple authorship, exerted over considerable time, similar in that sense to the epic's own account of composition. They generally postulate that the epic began with oral storytellers and performers relating heroic tales that perhaps (although not necessarily) looked back to some long-past historical dispute. Perhaps there was a battle between rival Indo-Aryan clans around 900 BCE that formed the initial kernel for the epic narrative, but the stories gradually departed from any concern with historical veracity and took on their own narrative reality. These transmissions were eventually gathered together and formed into a single central story, with many digressions and ancillary materials, which at some point was committed to a written version. But when and why did this epic consolidation take place?

Recent scholarship on the *Mahabharata* has emphasized that religious and political developments in classical India provided a powerful impetus for the transformation of old stories of ancient Kshatriya battles into a vast new epic narrative.[4] Notably, the rise of Buddhism and Jainism—renunciatory movements that explicitly denied

Vedic and brahmanic authority—posed a powerful ideological challenge for proponents of orthodox traditions. The rise of the Mauryan dynasty (ca. 323–185 BCE), which united much of the subcontinent under a single imperial rule, also raised new questions, particularly when emperors like Ashoka Maurya patronized Buddhist institutions over brahmanic ones. In response to this fundamental challenge to Vedic and brahmanic authority, the authors of the *Mahabharata* sought to articulate a new vision of proper royal rule grounded on a modified Vedic tradition. This perspective suggests that the sponsorship for composing the epic may well have come from a post-Mauryan royal dynasty like the Shungas, who overthrew Mauryan rule in 185 BCE and explicitly sought to restore the preeminence of orthodox brahmanic practices, or the Kanvas who replaced the Shungas and ruled until 28 BCE.

Among recent scholars, James Fitzgerald postulates an initial shorter and porous work, a proto-*Bharata* composed during the Shunga period and subsequently expanded over the next several centuries. Somewhat later, perhaps under the imperial Guptas (320–497 CE), in Fitzgerald's view, an authoritative written redaction of the *Mahabharata* was finalized. This Gupta period work, promulgated widely, became the archetype for all the lineages of manuscripts that exist today. When Indian scholars working at the Bhandarkar Oriental Research Institute in Pune, India, from the early 1920s to the mid-1960s extracted a critical edition from the hundreds of available manuscripts, their edition probably approximated the written Gupta version.[5] Alf Hiltebeitel proposes a revisionist hypothesis, by which the composition of the entire epic, much as we have it now, occupied a relatively brief time. He envisions an interdisciplinary compositional committee of brahmanic intellectuals, working perhaps under the royal patronage of the Shungas or other orthodox kings.

Indological scholars have also debated the compositional relationship between the *Bhagavad Gita* and *Mahabharata*. Some have viewed the *Gita* as an extrinsic interpolation into the epic story. Franklin Edgerton speaks of the "dramatic absurdity" of this long conversational pause at the onset of battle. Most recent scholars, however, see the *Gita* an integral portion of the *Mahabharata*. In the introduction to his translation, J.A.B. Van Buitenen argues persuasively for this position.

> The *Bhagavadgita* was conceived and created in the context of the *Mahabharata*. It was not an independent text that somehow wandered into the epic. On the contrary, it was conceived and developed to bring to a climax and solution the dharmic dilemma of a war which was both just and pernicious. The dilemma was by no means new to the epic, nor is it ever satisfactorily resolved there, yet the *Gita* provides a unique religious and philosophical context in which it can be faced, recognized, and dealt with.[6]

Responding to the moral issues of war raised within the epic narrative, Brahmin poets developed a dialogue between principal characters at a moment of high tension in the story, and used it not only to deal with the dharmic dilemma of a fratricidal war but also to present a new vision of Krishna as Supreme Deity and outline a new form of religious devotional practice.

There is still one more way to answer the question of composition. The *Bhagavad Gita* was not just composed once and for all when Krishna spoke it to Arjuna, when Vyasa taught it to Vaishampayana, when Brahmin poets developed it under the patronage of the Shungas, or when Gupta rulers promulgated an authoritative written edition. In a sense, all new listeners or readers who engage seriously with the *Bhagavad Gita*, bringing their own concerns and aims to their readings, compose the work anew. The *Gita* is rich enough, complex and ambiguous enough, to give rise to many new compositions. In most cases these compositions take place just in the consciousness of the reader, in dialogues between reader and text, or in unrecorded conversations. In some, though, they take permanent form as written interpretations, commentaries, discourses, or translations of the *Gita*. We can recover the continuing life of the *Bhagavad Gita* over the centuries from these new *Gita*-based compositions.

Krishna and His *Gita* in Medieval India

CHAPTER 2

[Krishna said:] "There are many persons who have been freed of all passion, fear, anger, and have become purified through the austerity of knowledge. Filled with me, finding refuge in me, they have come into my being. In whatever way people seek me, in that same way I share in them. For humans, in all their various ways, follow the path to me, Arjuna."

—*Bhagavad Gita 4.10–11*

In the *Bhagavad Gita*, Krishna displays his own doubleness. He appears as a human friend and charioteer to Arjuna, and then he describes himself as a god and allows Arjuna to see the full extent of his divinity. Krishna proclaims himself to be the highest goal for devotional aspiration. Those who take refuge fully in him, he says, come to share in his being. In medieval India, Krishna did indeed become the center of a widespread and vigorous devotional cult. Yet it was not his role as Arjuna's instructor at Kurukshetra or as a princely figure in the *Mahabharata* that held the greatest attraction for medieval Krishna devotees. Rather, Hindu devotion toward Krishna focused primarily on his early life, when he was growing up in a tribe of rural cowherders, as a charmingly rambunctious infant and seductive flute-playing youth. Stories and poems celebrating this side of Krishna's biography circulated widely, eclipsing for most devotees the more formidable grown-up teacher of the *Gita*.

This is not to say that the *Bhagavad Gita* was forgotten in medieval times, but its audience seems to have been a more circumscribed and erudite one. The *Gita* circulated as an independent work, detached from the larger *Mahabharata* narrative. It was influential enough to inspire other gitas, in which other Hindu deities presented their own competing claims to supremacy. Religious philosophers, especially in the orthodox philosophical school known as Vedanta, commented on the *Gita*, often with sharply differing readings of Krishna's teachings. The *Bhagavad Gita* became an interpretive battlefield, a Kurukshetra for medieval theologians. And in Maharashtra, the devotional poet Jnanadeva composed a lengthy new work that translated and expanded on the Sanskrit *Gita* in the Marathi language.

From Krishna's own perspective, following the principle of inclusivity that he articulates in the *Gita*, these may all be seen as the "various ways" that different people in medieval India "followed the path" to God. Krishna appears to humans in many guises, as he suggests in the *Gita*. If some want to focus their religious efforts on loving Krishna as an adorable baby or alluring youth, this may be as acceptable and effective as seeking to put into practice his more challenging directives as an adult guide in the *Gita*. For us, tracing the biography of this wide-ranging religious work, they all warrant attention as episodes in the continuing life of the text.[1]

Krishna's Early Life and the Culture of Devotion

Characters in the *Mahabharata* are aware that Krishna, before assuming the throne in Dvaraka, has had an unusual upbringing for a king. In one dramatic scene early in the story, King Shishupala of Chedi loudly berates Krishna in a royal assembly for his humble background. How can a cowherder be honored as a king? It would be like marriage for a eunuch or a visual spectacle for a blind person, he charges. Fierce arguments break out among the rulers. Shishupala continues his diatribe, but when he finally insults Krishna one too many times, Krishna suddenly hurls his razor-sharp discus and neatly beheads the challenger. This quickly silences Shishupala, but not before his challenge raises the question of Krishna's shady past.[2]

Evidently there were many interested in this question, for a large new work, the *Harivamsha*, presented itself as a supplement (*khila*) to the *Mahabharata*, to relate the story of Krishna (Hari) and his lineage (*vamsha*). It was the prequel for the most intriguing character in the epic. Over the succeeding centuries, the life of Krishna would be retold, with variations, in numerous works such as the *Vishnu Purana* and *Brahma Purana*. The most influential of these was the *Bhagavata Purana*, a scripture of perhaps the ninth century, which retells the Krishna biography with a potent combination of theological sophistication and devotional fervor.[3] This is one of the seminal works in the Hindu tradition, deserving a biography of its own. The lengthy poem solidified the legendary biography of Krishna and provided a point of departure for myriad further developments in Krishna devotionalism. The *Bhagavata Purana*, in its telling of the early life of Krishna, illustrates and amplifies many of Krishna's key points in the *Bhagavad Gita*, but also pushes some of these teachings in new directions.

Krishna was indeed raised among a tribe of cow-herders, just as Shishupala charges, yet there is a back-story to that too. As the *Bhagavata Purana* relates, a host of demons have descended to earth. One of them, Kamsa, usurps the throne of Mathura from the rightful ruler, Ugrasena. The gods decide that this overturning of proper order requires divine intervention, and the god Vishnu incarnates himself in Mathura as Krishna, the human son of Devaki and Vasudeva. In the *Bhagavata* version, Devaki is the daughter of Ugrasena's brother, so Krishna's parents are part of the Mathura royal family. Unfortunately, Kamsa learns of the divine plan to remove him from the throne. He places Devaki under house arrest and murders each of her offspring as soon as they are born. Finally, when Devaki delivers the baby Krishna, her husband conceals the newborn, escapes from the palace, crosses the Yamuna River, and switches Krishna with another baby just born to Yashoda and Nanda, members of a nomadic tribe that pastures its cattle in the Vraja region outside Mathura.

Krishna thus grows up among the Vraja pastoralists doubly disguised: as a prince among cowherds and a god among humans. Even as an infant, Krishna periodically exhibits extraordinary powers. Although sometimes they seem like strange random events, most of his actions serve to defend Krishna and his adopted tribe from demons. From Mathura, the demonic Kamsa sends hench demons to get rid of the threat. By fending off these aggressive demonic attacks on the cowherd tribe in Vraja, Krishna gradually becomes the powerful protector of his people. Eventually, as a young man, Krishna returns to Mathura, where he kills Kamsa, releases his own parents from captivity, and returns the kingdom to Ugrasena.

The story of Krishna's deeds as a demon-killing youth, protecting his tribe and restoring proper rule in Mathura, fits well with Krishna's explanation of the purpose for his incarnation in the *Bhagavad Gita*. There has certainly been a "decline in righteousness and an increase in unrighteousness" in and around Mathura, and Krishna therefore takes a human form in order to restore dharma. Nevertheless, the *Bhagavata Purana* also focuses on another side of his life. The poem describes in loving detail the warm maternal love that foster mother Yashoda feels for baby Krishna, the close loving friendship that his boyhood playmates come to share with Krishna, and the erotically charged passionate love that overwhelms the Gopis (or cowherd women) as Krishna grows into adolescence. Even without recognizing Krishna's divinity, they come to feel an intense emotional devotion to the human Krishna living in their midst. This gives a new dimension to bhakti.

Drawing on the *Gita*'s teachings, the *Bhagavata Purana* forcefully reiterates the superiority of bhakti over other forms of religious practice. By placing Krishna in a tribe of cowherders, a marginal community clearly inferior in the social hierarchy to the Brahmins and Kshatriyas who populate the *Mahabharata*, the *Bhagavata* dramatically portrays the social inclusiveness of bhakti. Going a step further, the *Bhagavata* grants the greatest devotional roles to females—namely, Yashoda and the Gopis—and thereby gives emphatic support to Krishna's statement in the *Gita* that bhakti is a path available to all.

The style of bhakti that Krishna advocates in the *Bhagavad Gita*, however, is not quite the same as the bhakti portrayed in the *Bhagavata Purana*. As one scholar puts it, the "intellectual bhakti" of the *Gita* differs significantly from the "emotional bhakti" of the *Bhagavata*.[4] The *Gita* emphasizes that recognition of Krishna's divine nature is the foundation for devotion. For the cowherders of Vraja, by contrast, devotion to Krishna arises whether or not they apprehend his divine character. Most of the time they do not. But the love they direct toward the Krishna that they perceive as a human child, friend, or lover qualifies as bhakti. In fact, the *Bhagavata* suggests that recognizing Krishna to be God may even act as a deterrent to devotion. It might create an emotional distance between human and divine, and weaken the intimacy of the human-to-human relationship. A lack of recognition enables the cowherders to experience the highest bliss of direct and loving participation in

Krishna's being. This emotional intimacy may even trump conventional codes of proper conduct.

Near the end of the conversation in the *Bhagavad Gita*, after discussing the ins and outs of dharma at length, Krishna points to one escape clause to duty. If Arjuna holds Krishna firmly in his heart and takes refuge in him, he may abandon all his duties; God will liberate him from all sin (18.62–66). The *Bhagavata* takes this passage seriously indeed, and dramatizes it in the persons of the Gopis. These women may be wives and mothers with dharmic responsibilities to their husbands and children, but when Krishna plays his flute in the autumn woods, they drop everything they are doing to be with him. Once there, Krishna flirts, strokes, embraces, and pleasures the women. The *Bhagavata* does not condemn their derelictions of female dharma. Instead, it suggests that their willingness to transgress all worldly bonds in order to gain full intimacy with Krishna should be taken as a devotional paradigm. In the *Bhagavata*'s scale of values, we should all aspire to be Gopis. The human soul too may be called on to give up all worldly attachments to achieve that higher goal of sharing in God.

In the *Gita*, Krishna observes that devotion has the capacity to rehabilitate even criminals and sinners (9.30). The *Bhagavata* dramatizes the great salvific power of bhakti. Not just those who direct their love toward Krishna, but even those who focus on him with animosity or hatred also find themselves delivered. Even the demonic Kamsa attains redemption when killed by Krishna, the *Bhagavata* relates. Whenever Kamsa drinks, eats,

walks, sleeps, or breathes, he is thinking about his neme-
sis. His obsessive fear and hatred toward Krishna are his
salvation. Any immersion in Krishna, even with hostile
intent, is good bhakti. The generous and inclusive path of
devotion that Krishna first paved in the *Bhagavad Gita*
grows wider still in the *Bhagavata Purana*.

Yashoda, the Gopis, others of the cowherd tribe, and
even demons like Kamsa were fortunate to live in a time
and place where they could interact directly with
Krishna, the embodied God on earth. What about the
rest of us? The *Bhagavata Purana* presents itself as a sub-
stitute for Krishna's incarnate presence. In its concluding
verse, it states that anyone born after the departure of
Krishna from his incarnation who interacts with the
Bhagavata with an attitude of devotion can gain the same
salvation as those who lived with him during his earthly
life. Reciting or retelling Krishna's deeds as narrated in
the *Bhagavata*, hearing or reading them, or thinking
about or meditating on them all enable new audiences to
reenact the same states of mind and emotions for themselves that the characters within the *Bhagavata* experience. The story of Krishna, then, is not just a historical
narrative; the *Bhagavata* claims that it has permanent
resonance. Evidently many in medieval India agreed.

The *Bhagavata*'s narration of the early life of Krishna
among the cowherds and its expansive conception of
Krishna-bhakti formed the basis for a profusion of devotional literature as well as religious activity throughout the
subcontinent. What was the place of the *Bhagavad Gita* in
this lively culture of medieval Krishna devotionalism? To

judge by physical evidence, perhaps only a small one. One index is religious sculpture of the period. John S. Hawley surveyed eight hundred panels of Indian sculpture dating from 500 to 1500 CE in which Krishna has been identified as the subject.[5] Of these, only three refer clearly to the scene of the *Gita*, and just a few more depict scenes from the *Mahabharata* more broadly. Almost without exception the sculptors concentrate on Krishna's youthful exploits, as narrated in the *Bhagavata Purana*. By far the most common themes are his victory over the snake Kaliya and his raising of Mount Govardhana. Nor did the *Gita* lend itself to dramatic reenactments in the way that the early life of Krishna gave rise to a genre of dance dramas like the Rasa-lilas. The Krishnaite devotional poets did not take the *Gita* as a point of departure for their new songs, much preferring the cowherd Krishna of Vraja to the teacher of Kurukshetra.

Other Gods' Gitas

Although the charioteer and teacher Krishna did not play a great role in this Krishnaite devotional movement, the text of his teachings did circulate in medieval India among some as an important independent work of religious philosophy. One sign of this is the proliferation of competitive gitas. Krishna's *Bhagavad Gita* was renowned enough to inspire other Hindu gods, or their followers, to propound their own divine songs.

In medieval India, Krishna was not the only god who sang. The gitas of other gods form a genre of religious poems embedded in the massive corpus of medieval literature called the Puranas (or "old traditions"). There is the *Ishvara Gita* of Shiva contained in the *Kurma Purana*, the *Shiva Gita* of the *Padma Purana*, the *Ganesha Gita* in the *Ganesha Purana*, the *Rama Gita* in the *Adhyatma Ramayana*, the *Brahma Gita* portion of the *Yogavashishta*, the *Devi Gita* sung by the Goddess in the *Devibhagavata Purana*, the *Yama Gita* in the *Agni Purana*, and numerous others. These gitas are similar in form to Krishna's, but they present distinct teachings and make competitive claims on behalf of the other deities who speak them.[6]

Like the *Bhagavad Gita*, the gitas of other gods appear as dialogues between the deities and one or more auditors, usually but not always human. In most cases the auditor approaches the deity in a state of doubt or despair, similar to that of Arjuna on the battlefield of Kurukshetra. At the start of the *Shiva Gita*, for instance, Rama is despondent after his wife, Sita, has been abducted by the demon Ravana, and he goes to the god Shiva for advice. These gitas always involve discourses conveyed from deities to listeners that constitute authoritative instruction on the fundamental nature of the world along with guidance for effective human conduct leading to worldly benefits and ultimately liberation. The instructions, however, differ from song to song, depending on the particular school of thought involved. So in the *Ishvara Gita*, Shiva sets forth the key teachings of the Shaiva Pashupata school. In each case the divine speaker persuades the listener of his or her preeminence as the Supreme Deity, subsuming or subordinating all other deities. The theological explication typically culminates in a visionary transformation, in which the audience gains a glimpse of the deity in a supernal form, parallel to Arjuna's vision of Vishvarupa Krishna in the *Bhagavad Gita*. In the *Ganesha Gita*, for example, the prince Varenya is granted the "eye of knowledge" that enables him to see Ganesha in his all-pervading form. Varenya becomes confused and terrified by what he sees, much as Arjuna does at Kurukshetra. By the end of the song, the listener has accepted the deity's teachings and goes on to carry out the advice in the world.

A generative religious work like the *Bhagavad Gita* may live on through its offspring, even quarrelsome and contentious ones. Undoubtedly the *Bhagavad Gita* served as the formal model for these other divine songs. But they were not simple imitations. While they implicitly acknowledged the importance of Krishna's song through their appropriation of its form and rhetoric, they also sought to displace Krishna and establish the superior stature of competing deities, such as Shiva, Ganesha, or the Goddess, who proclaimed new teachings for new audiences. These gitas of the other gods suggest the vigorous competition among the gods that was characteristic of medieval theistic Hinduism. In the end, though, it was the genre's progenitor—Krishna's initial *Gita*—that would enjoy the longest and most diverse life. There the competition would be one of interpretation.

Vedanta and the Gita of the Commentators

> Without any self-interest, but only with a desire to help
> all beings, [the Lord Krishna] taught the Vedic *dharma*
> to Arjuna, who was drowning in a great ocean of grief
> and confusion, in hopes that this *dharma*, when ac-
> cepted and put into practice by virtuous people, would
> spread widely. . . . Now this treatise called the *Gita*, which
> contains the concentrated essence of the meaning of all the
> Vedas, is difficult to understand. Even though many com-
> mentators have explained the meanings of each word, the
> meaning of its sentences, and its overall plan in an effort
> to make visible its true meaning, the general public still
> perceives the work as conveying multiple meanings, and
> very contradictory ones at that. Recognizing this situation,
> I will compose a succinct exposition of the *Gita*, in order
> to determine its meaning through discrimination.
>
> —*Bhagavadgitabh ashya, 1–2*

So Shankara, writing in the early ninth century CE, commences his commentary on the *Bhagavad Gita*.[7] As he points out, the *Gita's* message may contain the holy Vedas in condensed form and it may be beneficial to all, but it is not easy to understand. He observes that many teachers have already tried to explicate the text, yet in his view serious misapprehensions are still rife among the public. With the conviction that he can do better, Shankara proposes a succinct exposition that will make manifest what he considers the true purport of the *Bhagavad Gita*.

Shankara was not the first, nor would he be the last, to seek to determine the true meaning of this difficult text. Throughout the medieval period the *Bhagavad Gita* was taken, within certain learned circles, as an autonomous work that conveyed valuable philosophical and religious truth, and many teachers took on the task of writing commentaries to articulate that truth. A recent compilation lists 227 extant Sanskrit commentaries on the *Gita*, ranging from the time of Shankara throughout the medieval period and up to the present. Many of these commentaries, like that of Shankara, engendered their own subcommentaries.[8] The truth that the *Gita* conveyed was evidently up for grabs, as exponents of widely divergent schools of thought and practice found in the text validation for their own distinctive tenets.

Although the *Bhagavad Gita* was not part of the Vedic corpus, Shankara characterizes it as containing the "concentrated essence" of the meaning of the entire Veda. Many of the best-known commentaries on the *Gita*, including that of Shankara, belong to the philosophical school known as Vedanta. The term vedanta literally means "end of the Veda," and refers to the Upanishads as the final portion of the Vedic corpus. As mentioned earlier, it can also be taken as the "culmination of the Veda," in the sense that the teachings contained in the Upanishads are said to complete or bring to fruition the knowledge of the Vedas. Adherents to the Vedanta orientation, accordingly, share a fealty to the Veda tradition as an eternal revelation of Truth and appreciation for the integrative quest of the Upanishads. Shankara claims in the introduction to his commentary that the Vedic dharma is the "cause of the preservation of the worlds." All Vedantins would accept this statement, but just what that Vedic dharma comprises is not so certain.

Multiple philosophical positions are sheltered under the capacious umbrella of Vedanta. The distinct schools of Vedanta are identified by their ontological orientations. Shankara is the preeminent exponent of the Advaita (or nondualist) Vedanta, but there is also a Dvaita (dualist) school led by Madhva (1238–1317 CE), and a Vishishtadvaita (qualified nondualist) school whose most esteemed teacher is Ramanuja. Other Vedanta schools include the Dvaitadvaita (both dualist and nondualist), the Shabdadvaita (language nondualist), and Shuddhadvaita (pure nondualist).[9] From an early period, Vedanta philosophers selected the *Bhagavad Gita* as one of their key works for philosophical articulation. Along with the Upanishads and *Brahma Sutras* (also called *Vedanta Sutras*) of Badarayana, the *Gita* was considered part of the *prasthanatraya*, the three fundamental "points of departure" for any exponent of a Vedanta school. The assumption was that these foundational works together present a consistent and comprehensive perspective, answering all significant questions, and it was the task of the Vedanta exegete to discover and present that Vedic philosophy in a clear, systematic, and tenable manner. Major Vedantins like Shankara and Ramanuja composed commentaries on all three of these works.

In medieval India, the commentary was a remarkably prolific and consequential form of Sanskrit literary practice. As Gary Tubb and Emery Boose observe, "Works of commentary pervade the history of Sanskrit thought to a degree that is unparalleled in the writings of most other traditions."[10] Many ancient and classical texts were difficult to understand, as Shankara said of the *Bhagavad Gita*. Others were so succinct as to be virtually incomprehensible without a commentary, like Badarayana's *Brahma Sutras*. Such super-brief core works were intended for memorization by students, with the expectation that a teacher would then explain their meanings in oral or written form. In medieval times, commentaries served to bridge the gap in comprehension between the older texts and new audiences. Written commentaries are like transcriptions of the textual explications that particularly gifted teachers might convey to their pupils. For modern students of India, these written commentaries provide a window into the ways philosophical writers and readers in medieval India understood the *Bhagavad Gita*.

Medieval exponents of the Vedanta school formed an interpretive community. In their exegetical enterprise, they shared certain fundamental premises and strategies, and these common commitments were germane to the way they read the *Bhagavad Gita*. At the same time, the common premises supplied a foundation on which differences of interpretation could be raised, explored, and contested. Medieval Vedantins shared a fundamental commitment to the Vedic tradition and three textual points of departure, but they also disagreed vehemently over ontological and theological positions. Those ontological differences constitute the distinct major schools of thought within Vedanta: nondualist, qualified nondualist, dualist, and the rest.

Here we will briefly consider some shared premises of the Vedanta commentators as they apply to the *Gita*, and then some areas of irresolvable interpretive disagreement between the two best-known Vedanta authors, Shankara and Ramanuja. In Vedanta commentaries on the *Gita*, one major point of debate was theological. Who is Krishna, and more generally, what is the nature of God? How should readers understand the claim to supreme divinity that Krishna makes in the *Gita*? A second issue was soteriological. What different paths leading to a realization of the highest human aim does Krishna present in his teachings to Arjuna? Which of these is the most efficacious?

The Vedanta commentators recognize that the *Bhagavad Gita* is a portion of a larger text, the *Mahabharata*, which they view as a work of history, not as a fictive epic. Yet they consider the *Gita*, as a separable work, to have a special status greater than historical facticity. It is a revelation of truth. This status derives from the identity of the main speaker, Krishna, who is divine, though the precise nature and scope of that divinity is open to debate. Krishna's teachings in the *Gita* are not a unique revelation. The commentators also accept the special truthfulness of the Veda as a whole, and of the Upanishads in particular, considered as an eternal revelation of dharma not composed by any human (*apaurusheya*). They emphasize the three textual foundations as the authoritative basis for the full articulation of any philosophical perspective. Since the truth is unitary, these three basic texts must cohere with one another. As Shankara puts it, the *Gita* contains the concentrated essence of the Veda. The teachings of the *Gita* must be read in such a way that they do not contradict the Upanishads and *Brahma Sutras*. Any apparent disagreements among these core texts must be reconciled.

The truth taught by Krishna to Arjuna is not a transient or historical one but instead permanent and universal, according to the Vedantins. At the same time, the commentators recognize that human interpretations of the *Gita* are multiple, and so any commentarial presentation of the text must establish its own validity and authority in debate with other possible interpretations and viewpoints. The other views include even those who do not accept the authority of the Veda, such as Buddhists and Jains, as well as other contending Vedanta schools and other broadly Hindu perspectives. The commentators often represent opposing positions within their commentaries as "preliminary views," and then go on to refute or encompass those views and establish their own position as the "demonstrated conclusion."

Finally, Krishna's teachings in the *Bhagavad Gita* are not simply descriptive of the world. They are practical. They are intended to enable qualified humans to act in such a way that they gain maximum benefits, formulated most simply as the "Highest" (*sreyas*). The highest aim for all humans, either directly or eventually, is a state of freedom or liberation from all the bonds that inhibit one's full attainment. This also entails a freedom from all future transmigration in the cycle of existence. In Hindu writings, the most common term for this is moksha. Krishna's teachings to Arjuna set out various means to attain this highest end. Nevertheless, Vedantins disagree sharply on the best method of attaining this Highest.

Who is Krishna, the speaker of the *Gita*? All Vedanta commentators accept that Krishna is not merely a human character in the *Mahabharata* but rather a divine being. Yet what of the special claims Krishna makes in his discourse that he is in fact the Supreme Deity? In particular, Krishna identifies himself in the *Gita* as the brahman, the term that other foundational Vedanta works use most often to designate the Absolute.

For Ramanuja this poses no difficulty. He introduces his commentary on the *Gita* with an extended celebration of Vishnu Narayana as the Supreme Being.[11] This great Being is the "ocean of innumerable beautiful qualities, such as boundless and supreme knowledge, power, force, sovereignty, fortitude, master, and the like," and He is, says Ramanuja, the Supreme brahman and the Highest Person. In his highest form, Vishnu is inaccessible to the meditation or worship of humans or even other deities. By his own sovereign will, however, Vishnu repeatedly and generously assumes worldly shapes of all sorts, without giving up his essential nature. In such shapes, Ramanuja continues, "he has descended repeatedly to various worlds in order that He might be worshiped by the beings who live in those worlds and so bring them nearer the fruits of dharma."[12] Krishna is one of those human shapes assumed by Vishnu, an incarnation or avatara much as Krishna describes himself in the *Gita*, descending to support righteousness in the world. (In the *Bhagavad Gita* itself, Krishna does not specify that he is an incarnation of Vishnu.) In Ramanuja's two-sided formulation, Vishnu Narayana is at the same time transcendently Supreme and easily accessible. This fits well with the doubleness that Krishna himself describes in the *Gita*.

For Shankara, a strict nondualist, Krishna's assertions in the *Gita* are not so easy to accept. Shankara is strongly committed to the Upanishadic formulations of the brahman as an underlying, eternal, unitary Absolute without attributes (*nirguna*). The brahman is, in the famous apophatic passage from *Brihadaranyaka Upanishad*, "not this, not that." It cannot be qualified by any positive attribute. A human-formed being like Krishna could not possibly be the brahman, as defined in this way. He can only be, as Shankara sees it, a secondary or functional appearance of that brahman. Krishna appears as if embodied, as if born in the world, a kind of spectral projection of the brahman. Krishna's as-if-ness consigns him to a secondary status in Shankara's ontological order.

All Vedantins accept that human existence is in some basic way unsatisfactory. The purpose of Vedanta teaching is to ameliorate this condition. Vedantins begin from the premise that the central drama of human life revolves around the personal soul, living in the world in seeming alienation from the Supreme. This alienation is not fundamental or permanent. Both Shankara and Ramanuja affirm an underlying unity of human souls and the Absolute, and that unity is what must be regained. But the path toward recovery differs for the two Vedantin commentators, and this leads them to emphasize differing parts of Krishna's complex message in the *Bhagavad Gita*.

As we have seen, Krishna proposes multiple paths in the *Gita*, and the medieval commentators argue heatedly over which should be given priority. One early commentator's position, which Shankara cites as a preliminary view, is that Krishna advocates a path of "combined knowledge and action." This may have some limited worldly value, he admits, but Shankara firmly rejects this as a path leading to the Highest. For Shankara, the only truly efficacious path is that of knowledge. The basic problem is one of ignorance—a failure to recognize the true identity of oneself with the brahman. Liberation must come about through recognition of an already-existing state of affairs, an epistemological shift rather than any ontological transformation. One must overcome all the false projections, the things we think we know, that cause us to see a complex differentiated world where there is really only brahman. With the destruction of such ignorance comes liberation. For the nondualist, true knowledge consists not in knowing many things but instead in fully realizing just that one big thing.

Shankara insists not only that knowledge is superior to action as a means to religious attainment but also that true knowledge involves an abandonment of action. It is not enough to abandon one's attachment to the fruits of action, as Krishna appears to suggest in the *Gita*. One must renounce worldly action altogether and become a renouncer. So argues Shankara, who according to traditional accounts became a sannyasi by age seven without ever living as a householder. But this raises an interpretive quandary for Shankara, since in the *Gita*, Krishna forcefully urges Arjuna to engage in battle. Here, says Shankara, one must consider the identity of the auditor. Like any good teacher, Krishna adapts his message to his audience. Arjuna is a Kshatriya warrior and householder, not a Brahmin or renouncer. As a householder active in worldly affairs, he is not in a position to follow the highest path of knowledge, as Shankara sees it, which would require the renunciation of action. As a member of the Kshatriya class, Arjuna should not become a renouncer, which in Shankara's view is best undertaken only by Brahmins. Taking into account his friend's options, Krishna thoughtfully recommends methods by which Arjuna may act within his situation that will allow him to acquire the qualities necessary to eventual liberation, such as mental and emotional tranquillity. Krishna's provisional advice to Arjuna is meant to enable him to gain the mental purity with which, in some unspecified later lifetime, he can adopt the more truly effective path of renunciation and nondualist knowledge.

For Ramanuja, the path of knowledge alone will not suffice for higher ends. He in fact starts with a doctrine similar to the combined knowledge and action position that Shankara has earlier criticized. Knowledge and action work together. As a person gains in correct understanding of the self, interested action becomes disinterested. Over time one's knowledge and action become more and more integrated. No doubt this is a highly laudable state, and may even constitute a type of liberation. In Ramanuja's theological scale of forms, however, this can only be preparation for a still-higher level of attainment: the realization of God. That can only come about through the third of Krishna's three paths, the discipline of devotion. Krishna has come to the Kuru-kshetra battlefield, Ramanuja claims, precisely to reveal the new path of devotion as the means of gaining the highest state.

Full devotion to God leads to a state of oneness, from Ramanuja's vantage point, but it is a different kind of union than the one envisioned by Shankara. In both cases there is a realization of unity between a person's individual essence and the Absolute brahman, in which the individuality of the person is transcended. The final relationship between the single-minded devotee and Highest Person is, for Ramanuja, one of dependence, the unequal union of the formerly alienated part back into its completing Whole. In this relationship of divine dependence, the liberated devotee finds limitless joy.

Both Shankara and Ramanuja came from orthodox South Indian Brahmin families, and both remained deeply committed to the religious legacy of the Vedas. Within the broad perspective of the Vedanta, though, the two commentaries articulated divergent philosophical visions, and their readings of the *Bhagavad Gita* reflected those views. So too did Shankara's and Ramanuja's lives follow radically different paths. Shankara was a lifelong renouncer; Ramanuja lived for a time as a married householder. Shankara spent much of this life as an itinerant pilgrim; Ramanuja settled for many years as manager of the largest Vishnu temple in southern India. Ramanuja participated actively in the temple liturgy of the Ranganatha temple of Shrirangam, where Vishnu was worshipped in the material form of a great, sculpted image, and where the Lord was celebrated with the devotional hymns of the Tamil poet-saints. His devotional interpretation of the *Gita* was grounded in the temple culture of twelfth-century Tamilnad. A century later in Maharashtra, the devotional orientation of the *Gita* took on a different form, as itself an extended devotional hymn, in Jnanadeva's *Jnaneshvari*.

Jnanadeva and His Meta-*Gita*

In medieval India, the Sanskrit epic narratives *Mahabharata* and *Ramayana* were widely retold and rewritten in the many developing vernacular languages of South Asia. Often the new vernacular epics became the first or most prestigious literary works in these languages.[13] By and large the *Bhagavad Gita* did not lend itself to this kind of narrative metamorphosis. There is one great exception to this. In the thirteenth century, the poet-saint Jnanadeva composed an expanded Marathi-language version of the *Gita*, known as the *Bhavarthadipika* or more commonly the *Jnaneshvari*. This remarkable work is the earliest extant version of the *Gita* in any Indian vernacular language, and is widely considered the first major poetic work in literary Marathi.[14]

Jnanadeva was born in a Maharashtrian Brahmin family, but according to traditional biographies his father was cast out from the local Brahmin community, and the family led a peripatetic life while Jnanadeva was growing up. His older brother Nivrittinatha later became Jnana-deva's spiritual guide, and somewhere along the way Jnanadeva acquired enough learning to explicate for others a difficult Sanskrit work. At the start of his *Jnaneshvari*, Jnanadeva acknowledges that Sanskrit is hard. He aspires to make the teachings of the *Bhagavad Gita* accessible to an audience of ordinary Marathi speakers. Jnanadeva is not interested in a word-for-word philosophical exposition like those composed in Sanskrit by Vedantin commentators such as Shankara and Ramanuja. Nor is his work a translation aiming at faithfulness or fidelity to a fixed original source, as we often understand the goal of translation. Rather, the *Jnaneshvari* is a self-standing poetic composition in its own right, constructed over and around the *Bhagavad Gita*, as a kind of meta-*Gita*. The seven hundred verses of the Sanskrit *Gita* are embedded in a nine-thousand-verse Marathi poem that translates, paraphrases, explains, expands, and extols the teachings of Krishna. In the end, Jnanadeva suggests, the two compositions may merge into one another. "If a person carefully reads my Marathi version of the original Sanskrit *Gita* with a clear understanding of its meaning," he writes, "he cannot say which is the original. Because of the beauty of the body, it becomes an ornament to the very ornaments that it wears, and one cannot say which of the two beautifies the other" (132).

Like the *Mahabharata*, the *Jnaneshvari* presents itself as a dramatized oral performance in which other dialogues are embedded. To retell the conversation of Krishna and Arjuna at Kurukshetra, as retold by Sanjaya

FIGURE 3. *Shri Jnaneshvar* (Jnanadeva composing Jnaneshvari),
chromolithograph by Mulgaonkar, ca. 1960.
Published by Anant Sivaji Desai. Author's collection.

to Dhritarashtra, Jnanadeva presents himself before an audience at a holy site on the south bank of the Godavari River, with his own guru Nivrittinatha present, and performs his explication of the *Bhagavad Gita*. A scribe named Sacchittananda writes down his words. Jnanadeva addresses his immediate audience, and the audience listens attentively, sometimes interrupting the speaker to praise him or urge him to continue. Jnanadeva frequently pauses to praise his guru. Nivrittinatha also intervenes in his disciple's performance, usually to ask him impatiently to stop digressing and get to the point. In his oral discourse, Jnanadeva adopts the voices of all the characters of the *Gita*: Sanjaya, Dhritarashtra, Arjuna, and most of all Krishna. With Krishna, however, something more is involved. As Jnanadeva praises Krishna, he exclaims that Krishna has filled him up with Himself, so that his voice is wild with desire to praise Krishna. Jnanadeva loses his separate individuality and becomes suffused with Krishna. In this state of devotional participation, Jnanadeva gains the capacity to give voice to Krishna's teachings in this greatly expanded new *Gita*. Jnanadeva understands himself as a channel for the god Krishna himself to repeat and expand on his earlier teachings in the Sanskrit *Bhagavad Gita*, now updated for medieval Maharashtra and delivered in the Marathi language.

Like the Vedanta commentators, Jnanadeva considers the *Bhagavad Gita* to convey the essence of the Vedas. It is divine ghee, he says, churned from the ocean of the Vedas, then heated in the fire of wisdom and boiled to perfection through discrimination. The *Gita* also reveals the essence of the *Mahabharata*, he contends. He compares the *Gita* to a city, within whose seven-hundred-verse walls all the scriptures have come to dwell harmoniously. But Jnanadeva does not view the *Gita* as a completed or closed text, composed once and for all at some moment in the past. In Jnanadeva's mind, Krishna is a living god still active and speaking in the world. The *Jnaneshvari* therefore allows Krishna to expand and update his original teachings of the *Gita*. He explains terms and ideas with profuse new metaphors and analogies. Moreover, Krishna now discusses new ideas and new practices that had not been part of the religious world of classical India. He urges the repetition of God's names, *nama-japa*, for example—a new devotional practice in Jnanadeva's medieval community. In the *Jnaneshvari*, Krishna explains in detail the new yogic disciplines of the Natha school, involving new concepts of the subtle body and awakening of Kundalini. Jnanadeva suggests that Krishna is here acting like a shopkeeper who brings out the special items previously kept hidden to show to favored customers. If the *Gita* is Krishna's store, it must include his new as well as old merchandise.

While acknowledging and praising all the paths of spiritual advancement in the *Gita* (and some added since then), Jnanadeva grants the greatest praise to bhakti. He observes that bhakti is an inclusive religious pathway open to members of all social classes, both male and female. In the *Jnaneshvari*, the style of bhakti proclaimed is closer to the fervent emotional devotion of the *Bhagavata Purana* than to the intellectual bhakti of the *Gita*.

Jnanadeva refers occasionally to Krishna's earlier life among the cowherds of Vraja, but that is not his main concern. Rather, he seeks to recast the relationship between Krishna and Arjuna in more intimate terms. He stresses the love that Arjuna feels toward Krishna, and reciprocally Krishna's love toward Arjuna. Most important, this reciprocal love of human and God does not rest on a fundamental separateness. Jnanadeva recognizes that true devotion leads to a merging or union with Krishna. Jnanadeva is a nondualist like Shankara, but unlike the Advaitin, he is a theistic and devotional one.

Not content simply to assert this philosophical nondualism, Jnanadeva transforms the *Gita* into a narrative of movement from separateness to oneness and then back again to separation. The dialogue of the *Gita*, in Jnanadeva's telling, involves not just Krishna's teachings on spiritual attainment but also their practical realization in Arjuna's experience. Near the conclusion of the conversation, in the *Jnaneshvari*, Krishna declares that his love for Arjuna does not arise from their separation. They are one. Then going beyond verbal instruction, he hugs his friend.

> Then stretching out His right arm, dark-skinned and adorned with bracelets, He embraces His beloved devotee who had come to Him. That high state of union from which speech, unable to reach it, turns back taking the intellect with it, and which neither word nor thought can attain, this was the experience into which Krishna drew Arjuna under the pretext of this embrace. (338)

In this experience of union, beyond words and thought, a flood of joy overwhelms Arjuna, and also (since they are one) submerges Krishna. As with Arjuna's vision of Krishna's supernal form in the *Gita*, this direct state of merging does not last. Krishna restores Arjuna's sense of separateness. Arjuna realizes he is Arjuna, wipes away his sweat and tears of joy, and steadies his voice to speak again to Krishna. That sense of provisional separation from God is the condition necessary for Arjuna to act in the world and carry out his services for Krishna.

Jnanadeva compares the *Bhagavad Gita* to the mythical wish-granting gem Chintamani. Like that famous multifaceted jewel, he says, the *Gita* provides a wide range of meanings and satisfies the many differing desires of its varied audiences. Shankara saw this multiplicity of meanings as a problem that he hoped to overcome with a persuasive commentary. Jnanadeva remained closer perhaps to the ethos of the *Gita* itself, where Krishna promises to share in them "in whatever way people seek me." And his idea of the Chintamani, with its many facets sending out beams in every direction, offers an apt metaphor for the contentious life of the *Bhagavad Gita* in medieval India. It fits as well the continuing biography of the *Gita* in colonial and modern times, as it would come to send its new rays of light throughout both India and, across the ocean, the world.

Passages from India

CHAPTER 3

In 1866, the transatlantic undersea cable was laid across the Atlantic Ocean, electrically linking the United States with England for telegraphic communication. In 1869 the Union Pacific and Central Pacific lines were joined in Utah with a golden spike to complete the transcontinental railway across North America. That same year, the French Suez Canal Company opened its canal linking the waters of the Mediterranean Sea and Indian Ocean, significantly reducing transportation time between Europe and Asia. In New York, Walt Whitman celebrated this confluence of human earth-spanning accomplishments in his poem of 1871, "Passage to India."[1]

> Singing my days,
> Singing the great achievements of the present,
> Singing the strong light works of engineers,
> Our modern wonders, (the antique ponderous Seven
>   outvied,)

In the Old World the east the Suez canal,
The New by its mighty railroad spann'd,
The seas inlaid with eloquent gentle wires

In Whitman's embracing vision, these great feats of engineering also span time. They will bring the ancient worlds with their great fables and spiritual truths, embodied for Whitman in India, into his modern North American world, or enable his embodied soul to journey back to ancient India. He honors not just the works of modern science but also

myths and fables of eld, Asia's, Africa's fables,
The far-darting beams of the spirit, the unloos'd
    dreams,
The deep-diving bibles and legends,
The daring plots of the poets, the elder religions

Addressing his own soul, Whitman suggests that these great unifications of space and time are in fact God's own plan.

Passage to India!
Lo, soul, seest thou not God's purpose from the first?
The earth to be spann'd, connected by network,
The races, neighbors, to marry and be given in
    marriage,
The oceans to be cross'd, the distant brought near,
The lands to be welded together.

Through such spatial and temporal passages, the ancient Indian "bibles" like the *Bhagavad Gita* with their "far-darting beams" can take on new forms, in new places, for new readers beyond India.

Whitman does not mention the *Bhagavad Gita* by name in "Passage to India," but it certainly was one of those Asian bibles that he had in mind. He noted that in preparation for composing *Leaves of Grass*, he read "the ancient Hindoo poems," and when the first edition of *Leaves* was published, Ralph Waldo Emerson commented that it read like "a mixture of the *Bhagavat Ghita* and the New York *Herald*." When Whitman died, it was reported, a translation of the *Gita* was found lying under his pillow.[2]

The *Bhagavad Gita* did not have to pass through the Suez Canal or across the transatlantic cable to reach Whitman. It was already in New York well before the 1860s. We can trace some of the earlier earth-spanning actions that brought this ancient Indian work to the attention of Whitman as well as other US and European readers in the late eighteenth and nineteenth centuries. The first was an act of linguistic passage: the translation from classical Sanskrit to modern English. Once the *Gita* and other unfamiliar works from ancient India arrived in Europe, their new readers had to find ways to accommodate them within existing Western ways of knowing the world.

First translated into English in 1785, the *Bhagavad Gita* was repeatedly proclaimed to be the foremost work of Hindu religious philosophy and subsequently gained the title of the "Hindu Bible." As a result, the *Gita* figured prominently in European discourse about Hinduism and

India in the late eighteenth and early nineteenth centuries, often as a synecdoche for India itself. It was the Kurukshetra on which European intelligentsia battled over how to understand Indian culture and its deep past. In a period of European expansionism and the British acquisition of colonial control over South Asia, debates over this ancient text frequently took on a decidedly contemporary political valence.

The same globalizing processes that brought the *Gita* as an ancient Hindu text to Europe and the United States at the end of the eighteenth century also brought living Hindu teachers by the end of the nineteenth. Starting with Swami Vivekananda's remarkable appearance in Chicago at the World's Parliament of Religions in 1893, Indian interpreters have exercised their powerful say to Western audiences about Hinduism, adopting the *Bhagavad Gita* as their central text. In this chapter we trace the *Gita*'s passages out of India, from its first English translation to Vivekananda's mission to the United States.

Charles Wilkins and His English *Gita*

In the 1840s and 1850s, as he prepared himself for a career as a poet, Whitman spent a great deal of time "loafing" in the libraries of New York. In the Astor Library (an ancestor of the New York Public Library) during that period were several translations of ancient Hindu poems available to the young Whitman. Among them was the English translation of the

Bhagavad Gita by Charles Wilkins, published in London in 1785. The *Gita* was in fact the first work of classical Sanskrit translated directly into English, and its appearance opened a Suez-like stream of works from ancient India on to the intellectual shores of Europe, including the *Hitopadesha* (1787), *Shakuntala* (1789), *Gita Govinda* (1792), the *Laws of Manu* (1794), and many others to follow. These works caused a sensation in European learned circles, and also reached across the Atlantic to make a powerful impact on North Americans like Emerson, Henry David Thoreau, and Whitman. But Wilkins's work depended on other earth-spanning forces, most immediately the establishment of British colonial control in eastern India, which brought the young English administrator into contact with learned Indian Brahmins.

Wilkins sailed from England to Calcutta in 1770, at age twenty-one, to take up an appointment with the East India Company as a "writer" or junior clerk.[3] A few years earlier, the British trading firm had gained administrative authority over a large portion of eastern India, and this was the starting point for its eventual colonial control over the entire Indian subcontinent. In 1772, Warren Hastings was appointed as the new governor-general for Bengal, charged with reforming corrupt Company practices. Soon after arriving in Calcutta, he issued his recommendation that the British colonial administration should seek to govern the territories under its control not according to British law but rather according to the laws and customs of the local residents. The first task for

Company officials, then, would be to determine what these laws actually were.

Hastings's proposal was the founding event of the Western discipline of Indology, for it led the British administrators of Bengal to the study of Sanskrit. The administrators were informed that the laws of the Hindu population were contained in codebooks called Dharmashastras, composed long ago in Sanskrit and promulgated by erudite Brahmin teachers or "pundits." (Another old Indic term adopted into modern English, the word pundit derives from the Sanskrit word *pandita*, "a learned person"). Hastings set about persuading the local pundits of Bengal to collaborate with British Company officials in compiling and translating the legal codes. This was not always an easy task, for many Brahmin pundits were rightly suspicious of the new foreign rulers. Others, however, found it profitable and perhaps stimulating to work with the new rajas, just as their forebears had adapted themselves to other regime changes in the past. The decision of some pundits to cooperate with the British opened the way for a few fortunate Englishmen to study Sanskrit.

Of all the British administrators under Hastings, Wilkins proved to be the most adept and highly motivated in his pursuit of Sanskrit learning. Around 1778, he later recalled, "my curiosity was excited by the example of my friend, Mr. Halhed [Nathaniel Brassey Halhed, who had tried unsuccessfully to learn Sanskrit], to commence the study of the *Sanskrit*. I was so fortunate as to find a *Pandit* of a liberal mind, sufficiently learned to assist me in the pursuit."[4] Wilkins does not mention the name of this pundit, whose "liberal mind" consisted of a willingness to collaborate with an English colonial official like Wilkins.

By 1783, Wilkins had made enough progress in his Sanskrit studies to begin translating the epic *Mahabharata*. He requested a leave of absence from his administrative duties in Calcutta, on health grounds, to travel

FIGURE 4. *Sir Charles Wilkins*, by James Godsell Middleton, engraved by John Sartain, ca. 1820.
© National Portrait Gallery, London.

to Benares No doubt he chose Benares not just for its healthful climate but more for the opportunity to work with Sanskrit pundits at the greatest center of traditional Hindu learning. Wilkins was "Sanskrit-mad," as the Indologist Henry Thomas Colebrooke later described his affliction. With Hastings's support, the Company granted the leave, and in early 1784 Wilkins relocated to Benares. There he met and worked with the pundit Kashinatha Bhattacharya, esteemed as a "master of every discipline of knowledge."[5]

At this earliest stage of Western Indology, British students of Sanskrit like Wilkins were altogether dependent on the vastly superior Sanskritic expertise of pundits like Kashinatha. There were no Sanskrit-English dictionaries, and no Sanskrit primers or grammars in any European language. There was none of the apparatus on which later generations of Western students have come to rely when learning Sanskrit. (Kashinatha himself compiled two such fundamental works for his British patrons Wilkins and William Jones: a list of Sanskrit verb roots and a ten-thousand-word vocabulary.) The British students also depended on the pundits for recommendations as to what texts to study and translate. Wilkins's choice to translate the *Bhagavad Gita* portion of the *Mahabharata* reflects the high value that his Brahmin pundits placed on the work. "The *Brahmans* esteem this work to contain all the grand mysteries of their religion," wrote Wilkins in his preface. Let us note that this statement represents the viewpoint not of all Hindus of all times but rather of a particular class of Sanskrit-teaching Brahmin pundits in northern India in the late eighteenth century. Generalizations of the *Gita* as the supposed bible of all Hindus would come later.

"Translation is treason," goes the adage, and it is always useful to be reminded that no translation is transparent. A translation can never fully reproduce an original. The greater the linguistic and cultural distance between the original and target languages, the wider is the gap that the translator must try to bridge. Every translation involves judgment and tactical choices. What does the translator (like any commentator or interpreter) see as the most fundamental significance of the original work? What aspects of the original work does the translator seek to convey, and what will one leave untranslated?

Wilkins makes no attempt to reproduce the poetical form, the metrical verse, of the Sanskrit *Gita* in his translation. He renders it in prose dialogue, though with enough King Jamesian "thees" and "thous"" to suggest a bible-like authority. His aim is to convey the meaning of the text insofar as he is able. He recognizes that his translation will not be entirely clear to English readers. He blames this not on cultural difference or on any imperfection in his own understanding of the text but instead on what he sees as the obscurity of the original.

The reader will have the liberality to excuse the obscurity of many passages, and the confusion of sentiments which runs through the whole, in its present form. It was the Translator's business to remove as much of this obscurity and confusion as his

knowledge and abilities would permit. This he hath
attempted in his Notes; but as he is conscious they
are still insufficient to remove the veil of mystery, he
begs leave to remark, in his own justification, that the
text is but imperfectly understood by the most
learned *Brahmans* of the present times; and that,
small as the work may appear, it has more comments
than the Revelations.[6]

Already in this first translation by an English student of
Sanskrit, Wilkins is criticizing his Brahmin teachers for
their imperfect understanding, a custom that would
persist through several generations of Indologists.

More interesting is Wilkins's judgment of the broader
significance of the *Bhagavad Gita*. He does not present
the work as an argument for a particular yogic discipline—
whether knowledge, devotion, or action—as its Indian
commentators often did. He does not give any indication
that he might see the application of Krishna's teachings to
his own life, as medieval Indian commentators had.
Rather, Wilkins locates the intention of the author as one
of religious reform within Hinduism.

> It seems as if the principal design of these dialogues
> was to unite all the prevailing modes of worship of
> those days; and by setting up the doctrine of the unity
> of the Godhead, in opposition to idolatrous sacri-
> fices, and the worship of images, to undermine the
> tenets inculcated by the *Veds*; . . . the design was to
> bring about the downfall of Polytheism; or, at least,
> to induce men to believe *God* present in every image

before which they bent, and the object of all their ceremonies and sacrifices.[7]

He views the *Gita*, then, as a historical document, valuable for the insight that it may yield about the early development of Hindu religion. This in turn may help his compatriots in understanding contemporary Hindu beliefs and practices, as part of a larger British project to comprehend the practices of their new colonial subjects, in order better to rule them. For many British observers, ancient texts like the *Gita* would enjoy priority over contemporary Indian informants in determining what would qualify as Hinduism. As Jones, his fellow Orientalist, put it, "[Those who wish to] form a correct idea of Indian religion and literature" should start by forgetting "all that has been written on the subject, by ancients or moderns, before the publication of the Gita."[8]

In October 1784 Hastings visited Benares on political business, and Wilkins took the opportunity to show his patron the *Gita* translation he had been working on. Hastings was delighted. As he wrote in a letter to his wife, "My friend Wilkins has lately made me a present of a most wonderful work of antiquity, and I am going to present it to the public."[9] By "public" Hastings meant not the local Indian one but rather the British public. He sent the manuscript by ship from Calcutta to London with a lengthy letter of recommendation addressed to his superior, Nathaniel Smith, chair of the East India Company board of directors. Hastings proposed that the Company publish this "specimen of the Literature, the Mythology, and Morality of the ancient Hindoos." To justify publication to the Company directors, Hastings argued that such learning held great value for the exercise of British colonial rule. "Every accumulation of knowledge," he wrote, "and especially such as is obtained by social communication with people over whom we exercise a dominion founded on the right of conquest, is useful to the state."[10] For Hastings and the East India Company, the translation of the *Bhagavad Gita* was a political act.

In May 1785, the work was printed under the title *The Bhagavat-Geeta, or Dialogues of Kreeshna and Arjoon; in Eighteen Lectures, with Notes*, translated from the Sanskrit by Wilkins. There is no mention of Kashinatha in the publication. In the "advertisement" that followed the title page of the book, the work is set forward, by virtue of its esteem within India and antiquity, as "one of the greatest curiosities ever presented to the literary world." The businesspeople of the Company board in London could not have anticipated how true this would prove to be.

Promise of the Primordial

Whitman was not the first person in the West to be thrilled by the Hindu poets or envision the possibility of finding some profound spiritual wisdom in the ancient bibles of Asia that could revivify the present. From the first appearance of Wilkins's rendering of the *Bhagavad Gita* in 1785, followed by other seminal translations from the Sanskrit, European savants looked to these newly available ancient works with avid excitement. Wilkins's translation was quickly translated into Russian and French, and a few years later into German. It was the time when the romantic movement was taking form in Europe, and an exalted image of India would hold an important position in the romantic sensibility.

The most enthusiastic reception took place in Germany.[11] Even before any Sanskrit works had appeared in Europe, the theologian Johann Gottfried Herder was portraying India as the cradle of civilization. Of the four ages of humankind, Herder speculated, the "childhood" of the human race took place in Asia, and he postulated that the inception of human culture must have occurred near the Ganges River. Inspired by Herder, the poet Novalis located the Garden of Eden somewhere in the Himalayas. India's language was more ancient, its mythology was older than any other, and wisdom itself seemed to have arisen on the Indian subcontinent. As Friedrich von Schlegel exuberantly proclaimed to his friend Ludwig Tieck, "Here is the actual source of all languages, all the thoughts and poems of the human spirit; everything, yes, everything without exception has its origin in India."[12] All these metaphors situated the Orient, and more specifically India, as the site of the primordial, in contrast to the European modern. For the German romantics, the primordial held a positive and compelling promise. They valued it as natural and pure, as opposed to the fractured and disenchanted reality of their contemporary European culture. In this reverse teleology, true perfection lay not in a future but instead at the very infancy of human culture. The original state of things could offer a critical perspective toward the present, an antidote to European traditions that these romantics viewed as moribund.

As it traveled from Benares to Calcutta to London to Germany, Wilkins's translation of the *Bhagavad Gita* landed in an intellectual field that was richly prepared for this old Indian poem. If the first stage of the human career took place in India, then Sanskrit works like the *Gita* could open a window into this ancient period of spiritual purity. The first incarnations of the *Bhagavad Gita* in the German language were secondary translations derived from Wilkins's English version. Herder translated portions of the poem, along with two other Indic texts, identified as representations of Indian brahmanic thought, in his *Zerstreute Blätter* of 1792. These Sanskrit works confirmed his great enthusiasm for all things Indian. But in rendering the *Gita's* thoughts, Herder extracted them from their textual setting and resituated them, along with excerpts from translations of the *Hitopadesha* and Bhartrihari's poetry, as epigrams in a topical scheme of his own devising.

The *Gita*, Herder declared, presents the great unitary premise of pantheism: One in all, and all into One. This is not simply a historical or culture-specific statement, as Herder sees it, but instead a universal theological principle with compelling ethical ramifications. All humans are quickened by the one World Spirit, and we should use our brief period of life to its best effect through reflection and conscientious actions. Humans ought to be led by reason, not by delusion or aversion. Truth, not error, should govern humanity. In contrast to Wilkins, Herder is not concerned with the history of Hinduism. Rather, in his view, Krishna speaks from the dawn of human culture to address perennial human concerns, just as applicable in late eighteenth-century Germany as in ancient India.

One of Herder's followers, Friedrich Maier, rendered the entire *Bhagavad Gita* from Wilkins's translation into German in 1802. While Maier located the *Gita* as one of the earliest expressions of the Hindu intellect, he also pointed to the analogies between many of its ideas and those of Plato, Benedict de Spinoza, and the Christian mystic Jacob Boehme. Other early European readers of the *Gita* similarly observed that the ancient Indian poet seemed to have anticipated and first articulated many tenets found in later Western philosophical or theological traditions. The French translator Jean-Denis Lanjuinais saw many such parallels. "It was a great surprise," he remarked, "to find among these fragments of an extremely ancient epic poem from India, along with the system of metempsychosis, a brilliant theory on the existence of God and the immortality of the soul, all the sublime doctrines of the Stoics, the pure love which bewildered Fénelon, a completely spiritual pantheism, and finally the vision of all-in-God upheld by Malebranche."[15] If India was the birthplace of human civilization, as the early romantic vision had it, then the *Bhagavad Gita* as one of its earliest written expressions could serve as the original wisdom book, containing the seeds of ideas that would come to fruition in the West in centuries to come.

The Supreme Romanticism, Abandoned

"We must seek the supreme romanticism in the Orient," declared the poet and literary critic Schlegel in 1800. Fired by his passion to discover a source of human wisdom that could restore European culture, Schlegel took up the study of Sanskrit in 1802. He was the first German to do so, and probably the first Westerner to learn Sanskrit without traveling to India or studying with an Indian pundit. His pundit was a retired British army officer and Orientalist, Alexander Hamilton, who had studied the language during his service in Calcutta. Hamilton was now in Paris cataloging the collection of Indian manuscripts in the Bibliothèque Nationale. At the time, the Scotsman Hamilton was the only person on continental Europe who knew Sanskrit, and he generously aided the German Schlegel in the French capital.[14]

By 1808 Schlegel issued the conclusions of his Indological studies, *Ueber die Sprache und Weisheit der Indier: Ein Beitrag zur Begründung der Alterthumskunde*, a lengthy comparative study of Indian language and philosophy. As an appendix to his book, he included direct translations from Sanskrit into German of extracts from the *Bhagavad Gita* and other important classical Indic texts. We should note how, in the European quest for

FIGURE 5. *Friedrich Schlegel*, painting by Franz Gareis, 1801. Public domain work of art from Wikimedia.

origins, "India" became confined here to its classical Sanskrit language and Hindu works of antiquity.

In his preface, Schlegel honors Wilkins, Jones, Hamilton, and other pioneers in the Western study of the Orient, and envisions the immense role such research can play in reinvigorating European thought.

> The study of Indian literature requires to be embraced by such students and patrons as in the fifteenth and sixteenth centuries suddenly kindled in Italy and

Germany an ardent appreciation of the beauty of classical learning, and in so short a time invested it with such prevailing importance, that the form of all wisdom and science, and almost of the world itself, was changed and renovated by the influence of that reawakened knowledge. I venture to predict that the Indian study, if embraced with equal energy, will prove no less grand and universal in its operation, and have no less influence on the sphere of European intelligence.[15]

Just as the rediscovery of Greek and Latin classics had provoked a renaissance in European intellectual life, so Schlegel predicts the study of Indian classics can catalyze a second and more profound rebirth—an "Oriental renaissance," as it would be later termed by Edgar Quinet and Raymond Schwab.

Expanding on the suggestions of Halhed, Jones, and others as to the lexical parallels between Sanskrit and other languages, Schlegel examined the grammatical systems of Sanskrit, Greek, Latin, Persian, and German, and demonstrated striking similarities among them. Ever in search of the primordial, he postulated that Sanskrit was the earliest form or source for the other languages. His linguistic work would inspire others like Franz Bopp, who went on to establish the discipline of historical philology, one of the seminal intellectual fields of the nineteenth century. His study of Indian languages also inspired his older brother, August Wilhelm von Schlegel, to move to Paris and study Sanskrit.

In the appendix to *Sprache und Weisheit*, Schlegel rendered about one-fifth of the *Gita* in metrical German. The pattern of his selections and omissions is significant. Schlegel avoids Krishna's instructions to Arjuna about work and duty, and also omits the teachings pertaining to the yoga of devotion. Much of the battlefield landscape drops out, as does Arjuna's vision of Krishna in his all-encompassing form. Instead, Schlegel highlights passages concerning the intellectual concept of the godhead and the human quest to find union with the divine. In short, Schlegel's abbreviated *Gita* is oriented around a *jnanayoga* interpretation, uncluttered by conflicting perspectives.

Despite the great impact that his work would have on others, Schlegel's own initial enthusiasm for ancient Indian literature as a direct source of wisdom waned over the course of his studies. During his writing of *Sprache und Weisheit*, Schlegel gradually came to believe that Christianity was not just one mythology among many in the world but rather provided the preeminent wisdom. He joined the Catholic Church in 1808, the same year that *Sprache und Weisheit* was published. From then on, he did not pursue any further studies of Sanskrit or Indian philosophy.

Within his newfound Catholicism, Schlegel had to find a way to locate the lesser wisdom of Indic works like the *Gita*. The earliest Indians, he proclaimed, had possessed knowledge of the true God. A primordial "glance" of revelation had fallen on India. In the course of time, however, this original wisdom had been overlaid with "a fearful and horrible superstition." Thus Indian religious thought followed a downward trajectory: the initial diffusion of the pure revelation degenerated in the direction of idolatry, astrology, and other Hindu abominations. In an early text like the *Bhagavad Gita*, Schlegel believed, glimmers of that ancient light of divine wisdom still could be glimpsed amid the unwieldy growth of erroneous mythology that had come to constitute Hinduism. The virtue of the *Gita* resulted from its antiquity along with its proximity to an original revelation, and Schlegel's selective translation highlighted the remnants of that divine manifestation. Yet unlike Hinduism, Catholicism had managed to preserve this revelation in its true form.

The 1808 work of Schlegel marks a significant moment of transition in the European study of the *Bhagavad Gita* and other classical Sanskrit works. Several divergent pathways proceeded from his studies. The romantic impulse with which Schlegel commenced his Sanskrit study continued, despite his own disappointed abdication. It took on a lively new incarnation across the Atlantic among the postcolonial transcendentalists in the United States like Emerson, Thoreau, Bronson Alcott (all enthusiastic readers of Wilkins's translation of the *Gita*), and Whitman. Thoreau took a borrowed copy of the Wilkins *Gita* with him to Walden Pond, where he imagined himself communing with a Brahmin priest on the Ganges as he sat reading at the pond bank.[16]

The nineteenth-century scientific study of Sanskrit and ancient Indic literature, in which German savants like Bopp and brother Wilhelm excelled, developed from Schlegel's comparative linguistic work and pioneering efforts at translation. In 1818, Wilhelm became the first academic professor of Sanskrit in Germany, at the University of Bonn. In 1823, he issued his own complete translation of the *Gita*, not into German, but into Latin, to give the old Indic text the aura of a proper classic. Wilhelm, not Friedrich, is often considered the real founder of Sanskrit studies in German. Between 1800 and 1823, the "supreme romanticism" that inspired the younger Friedrich had been supplanted by a new disciplinary ethos of the scientific study of Indian languages and texts. Even if India was not the source of a pure primordial revelation that Herder had envisioned, its ancient literature could still offer scholars an exciting new object for philological research.

Finally, with his Catholic resituating of the *Gita* as the corrupt residue of an original revelation, Schlegel pioneered the kind of critical reading that nineteenth-century Christians and especially missionaries working in India would give to the text: find the "good parts" that cohered with Christian doctrine, and dismiss the remainder as myth and superstition foisted by priests on a credulous native audience.[17] This fit with a broader narrative of India's historical degeneration, which would take firm root especially in British colonial discourse.

The Colonial Politics of *Gita* Reading

Nowadays, we readily accept that no reading of a work of religious literature is entirely innocent. Every reading draws on a reader's own presuppositions, values, and purposes. But some readings are less innocent than others. In late eighteenth- and early nineteenth-century Britain, those who read the *Bhagavad Gita*—as mediated through Wilkins's translation—did so in a political context. The broad issue was how the British were best to govern the new colonial territories on the subcontinent they had acquired by right of conquest. This debate rested on an evaluation of the society and institutions of the Indians. To what extent were Indians capable of self-governance? How directly and deeply should the British intervene in Indian society? Was Hinduism a positive or negative influence in the civilization of India? The *Bhagavad Gita* and other classical works translated from Sanskrit were taken as evidence for forming British judgments about contemporary India.

Governor-General Hastings and others in his early circle of Orientalists, enthusiasts for the products of Indian culture, believed that active British engagement in learning about India would aid the colonial enterprise by conciliating differences between rulers and ruled. As he wrote to the Company chair when advocating the publication of the *Gita* translation,

It is not very long since the inhabitants of India were considered by many [in England], as creatures scarce elevated above the degree of savage life; nor, I fear, is that prejudice yet wholly eradicated, though surely abated. Every instance which brings their real character home to observation will impress us with a more generous sense of feeling for their natural rights, and teach us to estimate them by the measure of our own. But such instances can only be obtained in their writings: and these will survive when the British dominion in India shall have long ceased to exist, and when the sources which it once yielded of wealth and power are lost to remembrance.[18]

It was the British attitude toward India that needed to change, according to Hastings, in order to ameliorate differences between the two peoples. He argued that reading the *Gita* would help a British public overcome its previous prejudice about Indian savagery, and acquire a more generous and true estimation of native dignity as well as accomplishment. Shifting to a broader historical perspective, Hastings closed with a prescient estimation of the relative duration of British colonial rule and the life of Indian writings like the *Bhagavad Gita*.

Hastings's generous outlook and conservative ruling strategy soon generated fierce opposition. The most formidable attacks came from two directions. Evangelical Christians like Charles Grant and secular utilitarians like James Mill found common cause in opposing the Orientalist orientation. Both began by emphasizing a profound difference between Indian and British societies on an evolutionary "scale of civilization." In the estimations of Grant and Mill, Indian society was indeed (as Hastings had put it) scarcely elevated above the savage level. The cause of Indian backwardness was not racial but rather cultural. Indians had been oppressed by their own political and religious despotism. Therefore, the great ruling task for the British in India, their moral duty, was "assimilation." For evangelicals and utilitarians, assimilation was not required of the British, as Hastings had suggested; it was up to Indians to become more like their new rulers. A profound transformation of Indian society was needed. Evangelicals and utilitarians differed on the instruments of transformation. Evangelicals naturally advocated a much greater role for Christian missionary activity on the subcontinent, while utilitarians put their faith in a more secular process of modernization. While both Grant and Mill gained influential positions within the East India Company, Mill exerted his greatest impact on the ethos of British colonial rule with his magnum opus, the *History of British India*, published in 1818.[19]

Mill was a thirty-two-year-old freelance journalist from Scotland living in London, trying to support a growing household that would eventually swell to nine children, when he began work on his *History of British India* in 1806. It might not have seemed the most obvious route to economic security for Mill to undertake a three-volume historical monograph that would take twelve years to write. Mill lacked any experience of living in India and had no training in any Indian language. Nevertheless, the project worked for him. When the *History* appeared in 1818, it was a great financial success, and the earnings helped sustain his family. Even better, the book established Mill as an authority on India, and he obtained a position with the East India Company in 1819, which he kept for the remainder of his career.

Mill calls his *History* a "critical history," by which he means a "judging history." In the preface he likens himself to a courtroom judge, sifting all the written evidence impartially to render judgment. His lack of any residential or linguistic expertise in India is a virtue, he argues, since it enables him to avoid any partisan perspective. One of the primary things this judge wishes to evaluate is the civilizations of the "Hindoos" and "Mahomedans" over which the British have acquired dominion. The items of evidence presented in Mill's historical court are the classical Sanskrit works translated into English by the Orientalists as well as various reports from travelers and missionaries in modern India. All are taken to represent a single Hindu civilization. The primary question to be decided is where these Hindus fit on a scale of civilization, an evolutionary continuum from the rudest savagery up to the most refined and exalted stages of humanity. Mill has no qualms in claiming the latter for the utilitarian judge himself.

Mill was certainly not an easy person to appear before. His eldest son, John Stuart Mill, who was subjected to his father's radical methods of home schooling during the years that Mill was working on the *History*, described his father's temper as "constitutionally irritable."[20] In the *History*, one can hear Mill bringing that same paternal impatience and irascibility to his evaluation of Hindu texts. In this case, though, his irritation was directed toward a clear political purpose. By demonstrating the childish backwardness of Indian society, Mill sought to persuade his British audience of the need for more forceful, transformative colonial intervention in native life.

Mill claims that religion plays a dominant role in Hindu civilization. "Every thing in Hindustan," he facetiously asserts, "was transacted by the Deity. . . . The astonishing exploits of the Divinity were endless in that sacred land." Accordingly, Mill's account of religion forms a central portion of his lengthy book 2, "Of the Hindus." The *Bhagavad Gita* figures significantly as a witness in this section of the *History*, along with the *Laws of Manu*, the Puranas, and missionary descriptions of contemporary Hindu practices. But none are allowed to appear as unified textual wholes. For Mill, the *Gita* does not exist as a narrative or part of the *Mahabharata*, and he does not bother with any attempt to comprehend Krishna's complex teaching as a whole. Rather, the *Gita* is a source of passages to be excerpted and juxtaposed with passages from other sources, other centuries, and other schools of thought. Let us take two examples from among the many where Mill deploys the *Bhagavad Gita* in his portrait of Hinduism.

In Mill's view, religion ought to provide a depiction of the cosmos as a connected, perfect system governed by general laws and directed toward benevolent ends. The Hindus fail grievously on this scale. "No people, how rude and ignorant soever, who have been so far advanced as to leave us memorials of their thoughts in writing, have ever drawn a more gross and disgusting picture of the universe, than what is prescribed in the writings of the Hindus."

Indulging his irritation with the childish Hindus, Mill continues, "All is disorder, caprice, passion, contest, portents, prodigies, violence, and deformity."[21] On what evidence does the judge base this assessment? Mill quotes the entire account of Arjuna's vision of Krishna's all-encompassing form at Kurukshetra as a "monstrous exhibition" of a guilty cosmology. He does not mention to his readers that this is a soldier's vision on a battlefield at the onset of a cataclysmic war, at a moment when those general laws of a perfect system have gone completely awry.

Hindu yogis come in for special contempt in Mill's account. Along with Manu's prescriptions for the renunciatory stage of life, Mill cites the *Gita* description of the sthitaprajna, the person whose wisdom is firm, as a proof text. These are the tortures that the religion of the Hindus requires. Moreover, he tells his readers, these Hindu yogis are required to renounce all moral duties and moral affections. Mill fails to notice that Krishna's depiction of the sthitaprajna is explicitly directed toward persons living in the world who wish to employ yogic techniques of self-mastery within their worldly activities. Nor does Mill mention the strong advocacy in Krishna's teachings to that worldly warrior Arjuna to observe dharma—that is, moral duty and moral affection—as a basis for proper impartial social action.

Mill's method of juridical interrogation has the desired outcome. "No coherent system of belief," he concludes, "seems capable of being extracted from their wild eulogies and legends."[22] Judgment is rendered. And since Hindu religion plays such a dominant and oppressive role in

India, according to Mill's portrait, the sentence must call for radical change. Mill did not seek the widespread Christianization of India, as Grant had, but rather a secular advancement in alignment with his utilitarian values. His position at the East Indian Company later allowed him to enact this agenda within Company policies. For the promise of ancient India to provide a primordial wisdom for benighted Europe, as the romantics hoped, Mill substituted the new nineteenth-century faith in universal progress, by which the rude Indian civilization would be led through Anglicization toward a more exalted destination.

Mill supplied an influential framework for those reading the *Bhagavad Gita*. If Indian commentators often highlighted especially powerful statements in the *Gita* for special attention as *mahavakyas* (great utterances), Mill sought out and isolated passages from the text that best supported his overarching pejorative vision of Hinduism. His *History of British India* became required reading for British personnel training for service in colonial India. Mill's selective decontextualizing method of reading set the horizon of expectations for other colonial period English readers approaching the *Gita* and other classical works.

The *Gita* and the *Geist*

Meanwhile in Germany, the *Bhagavad Gita* provided the field for a different kind of combat. As Wilhelm von Schlegel recognized, Germans did not have the same political and administrative motivation to learn about India that the British did. He maintained, though, that Germans did have a "special call to get to the bottom of Indian antiquity."[23] They could do this through the application of philological method and superior scholarly rigor. In the 1820s, Schlegel's Devanagari edition and Latin translation of the *Gita* provoked a series of arguments among German savants that would determine just where this bottom of Indian antiquity should be located. At stake in the debate were where India would fit in world history and where works of classical India like the *Gita* would be placed in a universal history of ideas that nineteenth-century Europeans were seeking to construct.

In explaining his choice of the *Bhagavad Gita* as his first Indic publication, Schlegel described the work as "a famous philosophical poem, praised in the whole of India, whose wisdom and sanctity can hardly be surpassed by any other." Whether true or not, Schlegel's comment reflected the European desire to find a single key to Indian religious thought, and reinforced the identification of the *Gita* as supplying it.

When Schlegel's work came out in 1823, it evoked some of the same fervor that had greeted Wilkins's English translation nearly four decades earlier. Wilhelm von Humboldt, the wide-ranging diplomat and linguist, wrote to Schlegel of his gratitude not just to the editor but also to destiny itself for giving him the opportunity to listen to the *Gita* in its original language. Like Whitman in the United States a few decades later, Humboldt was cognizant of the world-historical changes that enabled this ancient Sanskrit work to reach him in Germany. Not all shared the excitement, however. The French Sanskritist Alexandre Langlois published a strong criticism of Schlegel's translation in the new *Journal asiatique* in 1824. At issue was Schlegel's failure to find single translational terms in Latin for certain crucial Sanskrit terms in the *Gita*, such as yoga, dharma, and brahman.

Humboldt rushed to the defense of his friend Schlegel. In two lectures delivered in 1825 and 1826 at the Royal Prussian Academy of Sciences in Berlin, and later published in the academy's *Proceedings*, Humboldt proclaimed the *Gita* "the most beautiful, presumably the only real philosophical poem of all known literatures."[24] On the translation front, Humboldt observed that languages are not structured similarly. Consequently, an important Sanskrit word like yoga or dharma may have a semantic range that does not correspond precisely to any single term in Latin, German, or any other language. Translators, Humboldt contended, must leave themselves open to the multiple meanings inherent in the original and seek to render that fully. Moreover, he asserted, a work rich in philosophical ideas like the *Gita* must be approached as an integral whole, not by fitting it into a preexisting doctrinal category. "I furthermore hold," he continued, "that there is hardly another means to elucidate the numerous dark spots that still remain in Indian mythology and philosophy than to excerpt, one by one, each of the works which can pass as their main sources, and to investigate it completely and separately before comparing it with other works."

Humboldt, who was instrumental in establishing the University of Berlin (later renamed Humboldt University), was here setting out an agenda for the scientific, empirical, and philological approach to the study of Indian antiquity that his allies like Schlegel and Bopp were pioneering in the new German universities. The course of history, he believed, should only be investigated by means of a subtle, detailed study of the various peoples and nations of the world. The direction of history would be a matter of empirical inquiry, not a priori preconception. In this Humboldt was rejecting the reverse teleology of Herder and the romantics, who had looked to ancient India as a source of universal wisdom. At the same time, he was challenging the conception of history as the progressive self-manifestation of the *Weltgeist* or World Spirit, advocated by the Berlin professor of philosophy Georg Wilhelm Friedrich Hegel. Hegel rose to the challenge with two lengthy reviews of Humboldt's lectures on the *Gita*, which he published in his *Jahrbücher für wissenschaftliche Kritik* in 1827.[25]

Hegel's grand vision was centered on the movement of the remarkable *Geist* throughout human history. He viewed this as a single world-historical passage across time, connecting all human civilizations both East and West. Hegel shared the romantic premise that civilization had originated in the East. Yet he thought that this was not a privilege, for the East had remained mired in the early stages of the Spirit's movement. The primordial did not hold a promise of renewal, as the earlier romantics had imagined. As the Spirit spread from East to West, finally reaching Berlin, it had superseded its own earlier forms. In the temporal manifestation of the Spirit, as Hegel envisioned it, what is earlier comes to be encompassed and integrated into what succeeds those prior forms. The philosophy of the present already includes those of the past, and surpasses them. But why had the Spirit stopped in its tracks in India?

The task of Hegel's reading of the *Bhagavad Gita*, accordingly, was to demonstrate how its premises had contributed to the stultification of the Spirit in India. Following Wilkins, Schlegel, and Humboldt, Hegel portrays the *Gita* as expounding the basic essentials of the Hindu religion. By now, four decades after Wilkins's translation, Europeans had conferred a scriptural centrality on the *Gita* by repetition. Hegel further identifies the doctrine of yoga as "the essence of their religion as well as its most sublime concept of God." Hegel's depiction of yoga, however, is much narrower than the multifaceted explication that Krishna provides in the text. For Hegel, yoga requires a withdrawal and isolation from the world, leading to a passive immersion into the brahman. As the Hindu term for God, the brahman is a decidedly inert conception. Unlike the Christian God, Hegel contends, the Hindu brahman abdicates its divine obligation to engage in the world process. Somewhere along the line, Hegel has managed to neglect the fact that the interventionist Krishna proclaims himself the brahman, personally embodied on a real Indian battlefield, in order to persuade a warrior to engage in worldly combat. For Hegel, the introverted and static aspirations of Hinduism articulated in the *Gita* have consigned India to a backward status, lacking the dynamic agency of the West. India's political failure, its seemingly easy conquest by the British, is one consequence of its spiritual inertia.

If Mill and Hegel had had their way, the life of the *Bhagavad Gita* in the West, which had begun so optimistically with Wilkins's translation, Hastings's promotion, and the German romantic adoption, might have been squelched. For these influential writers, the *Gita* was best seen as a remnant of an earlier, obsolete stage of human development. But perhaps the *Geist* was moving in new directions that Hegel had not anticipated. Here and there the *Gita* was kept alive through the attentive readings of latter-day European romantics and US transcendentalists. Meanwhile, European scholars collecting and editing the works of the Indian past began to supply a fuller picture of the history of Indian religious thought and the place of the *Gita* within it. New versions began to appear by the latter half of the nineteenth century. The second English translation came in 1855, by J. Cockburn Thomson. The *Bhagavad Gita* reappeared twice in 1882, translated by John C. Davies and the erudite Indian jurist K. T. Telang, in the fifty-volume *Sacred Books of the East*, edited by F. Max Müller, the German Sanskritist and Oxford professor of comparative philology.

The *Gita*'s most popular new incarnation was Edwin Arnold's 1885 poetic rendering, *The Song Celestial*, which helped rescue its integrity for a new generation of readers. Although Arnold intended his work for an English audience, it had its most profound effect on the young Gandhi, studying law in London in the early 1890s. In that same decade, the first of many Hindu holy men made a passage to the West and began to present the *Bhagavad Gita* in a new, compelling framework to Western audiences.

A Hindu Swami at the World's Parliament

In his 1871 poem, Whitman imagined that the new technologies of transportation and communication would bring ancient bibles and legends to the United States. He did not envision in "Passage to India" that the same modern achievements might also bring living exponents of those still-living "elder religions" from India and Asia to his country. Yet in 1893, invited by transoceanic cables, and conveyed by canal, ocean liner, and transcontinental rail, came Buddhist, Jain, Hindu, and Parsee religious speakers to Chicago, where they represented their faiths to large and enthusiastic audiences at the World's Parliament of Religions, part of the World's Columbian Exposition. Whitman had died a year earlier, but it is pleasing to imagine how the poet might have lauded these dramatic Asian delegates, striking in their robes and turbans, sharing the great platform in the aptly named Hall of Columbus with the more familiar Christian reverends and priests. Of interest for us among these delegates was Swami Vivekananda, a Hindu delegate who created a great impression at the Parliament. The *Bhagavad Gita* served as a core text for his presentations there.

The Parliament of 1893 was itself a world-historical event in the history of religions.[26] Organizers saw it as an opportunity to display for American audiences the universal truth to be found in religion, and sought to identify and invite leaders from all the world's major religions to meet each other and present their doctrines in Chicago. Through articles in the Madras English-language newspaper the *Hindu*, word of the upcoming gathering reached Vivekananda, a follower of the Bengali saint Shri Ramakrishna. At the time he was living as a wandering mendicant in southern India. Somehow or other the swami developed the idea that traveling to the distant United States and speaking at this parliament might enable him to raise resources to aid in a plan he was formulating to alleviate poverty in India. Without any organizational affiliation, but with the encouragement of many friends in India and the material support of the Maharaja of Khatri, Vivekananda made the long voyage.

The itinerant Indian monk relied on new world-spanning technologies for his journey.[27] He sailed on a new trans-Pacific ocean liner, the RMS *Empress* of India, out of Bombay by way of Hong Kong and Japan to disembark in Vancouver, and from there he traveled across the North American continent on the newly completed Canadian Pacific Railway to Winnipeg, then on the Great Western Railway to Chicago. Arriving six weeks before the Parliament, Vivekananda journeyed to Massachusetts and then briefly reverted to his homeless mode of life on the streets of Chicago after his money ran out, until he was found sitting on a curb on North Dearborn Street, in an exclusive residential neighborhood. By miraculous good fortune, the Indian swami was spotted by Ellen Hale the day before the Parliament was to begin. "Sir, are you a representative to the World's Parliament of Religions?" she asked the exotic-looking visitor, and hustled him off to the home of Reverend John Barrows, the chair of the event.[28] Though Vivekananda arrived without any official invitation, several fortuitous chance meetings and his own persuasive personal qualities enabled him to gain admission as one of the delegates representing Hinduism. So it was that the young Hindu emissary marched in procession into the hall on September 11, 1893, with over sixty other delegates and seated himself on the dais. The first afternoon of the Parliament, he gave his opening remarks.

As soon as Vivekananda greeted the audience, "sisters and brothers of America," the crowd responded with a tumultuous ovation. The aim of the Parliament was to bring together representatives of the great religions of the world, and here in Chicago was a real Hindu holy man dressed in exotic orange robe and turban. The Parliament was not exactly an egalitarian assembly, however. The organizers were confident in the superiority of Christianity, especially in its liberal American Protestant form. One mark of this superiority, they supposed, was its tolerance of other faiths, as exemplified in this gathering. They expected the representatives of other religions, grateful to be included, to fit themselves into an evolutionary scale with Protestantism as its culmination. In his opening remarks, Vivekananda immediately laid claim to the virtue of tolerance on behalf of Hinduism. "I am proud to belong to a religion which has taught the world both tolerance and universal acceptance," he declared. "We believe not only in universal tolerance, but we accept all religions as true." This Parliament, he went on, could be seen as a fulfillment of Krishna's statement in the *Bhagavad Gita*: "Whosoever comes to Me, through whatever form, I reach him; all men are struggling through paths which in the end lead to Me."[29] The *Gita* was not a remnant of Indian backwardness or failure, as Mill or Hegel would have it, but rather a work of prescient modernity, anticipating the parliament. The swami had turned the tables on the organizers. Perhaps this parliament was not a demonstration of Christian superiority but conversely a new pathway by which North Americans too could struggle toward Krishna.

For Vivekananda, the *Bhagavad Gita* was a central text in the capacious living Hindu tradition. A few days later he sketched his view of this tradition for the Parliament audience in his "Paper on Hinduism." The foundation of Hinduism, according to Vivekananda, is the revelation found in the ancient Vedas, and the *Bhagavad Gita* is the most authoritative commentary on the Vedas. The Vedas proclaim that the spirit, which lives in the body, will go on living after bodily death, through transmigration into another bodily form. The central problem is that the pure and perfect spirit is imprisoned in matter. The aim must be to burst the bondage of matter and thereby enable the spirit to reach its divine perfection. This is the core of the Hindu system.

All this is taught by Krishna, Vivekananda continues, who Hindus believe to have been God incarnate on earth. Krishna is not just another parochial Hindu deity. As Krishna himself states in the *Gita* (according to Vivekananda's rendering), "I am in every religion as the thread through a string of pearls. Wherever thou seest extraordinary holiness and extraordinary power raising and purifying humanity, know that I am there." As Krishna is present in all religions, so salvation is available through many religious paths. One of the *Gita*'s main achievements, according to Vivekananda, is its reconciliation of different paths in classical India. Krishna's original insight, he observes, was that all these various spiritual disciplines could be seen as valid means to a common end. The same reconciliation could be applied, at the end of the nineteenth century, on a worldwide basis. Among the topics of debate before parliament delegates was the possibility of a future "universal religion." Vivekananda closes his lecture by endorsing the concept of a universal religion, but suggests it may already exist in the form of ancient Hinduism.

Vivekananda enjoyed tremendous success at the World's Parliament of Religions, and stayed on in the United States to become a traveling lecturer. A bureau organized a speaking tour for him. The exotic swami was a gifted orator as well as a curiosity, and attracted large

FIGURE 6. *Swami Vive Kananda, the Hindoo Monk of India*, poster, unknown artist, 1893.
Published by Goes Lithographic, Chicago. Reproduction courtesy Vedanta Society of Berkeley, CA. This poster was probably sponsored by Henry Slayton, organizer of Vivekananda's lecture tour.

audiences in cities in the United States, such as Iowa City, Des Moines, Minneapolis, Memphis, Detroit, and others. He promulgated his version of Hinduism, simplifying and adapting it for the American audience. From the *Gita*, he stressed two main themes he believed that most people in the United States needed. First is Krishna's tolerance of multiple paths toward spiritual attainment to counter the doctrinal rigidity he perceived in American Christianity of the time. Second was Krishna's principle of nonattachment to the fruits of action in order to temper the acquisitive materialistic ethos of the American gilded age. Along the way he made some strong criticisms of Christianity for its missionary practices in India. This embroiled Vivekananda in controversies with organizations in the United States that staunchly supported Christian missionaries in India. Finally he came to feel like "the chief attraction of a circus" and cut his ties with the lecture organizers.[30]

Rather than addressing crowds of the curious, Vivekananda turned his attention to attracting and instructing smaller groups of earnest seekers. For these select disciples, in the United States he taught private classes on the *Gita* and the Upanishads, and gave instruction in meditation. In 1894 he established the Vedanta Society of New York, and a similar society in San Francisco in 1900. These groups of American seekers, instructed by Vivekananda and other swamis from the Ramakrishna Order in India, became the first continuing Hindu organization in the United States.[31]

The swami returned to India in 1897. Thanks to Indian newspaper coverage of his exploits abroad, Vivekananda was welcomed as a hero who had achieved a great victory for Hinduism and India. But he brought back a message that India also had much to learn from the energetic West. In colonial India, he proclaimed, people had become lethargic and needed to recover the virtue of work. As he lectured an assembly in Madras, the *Bhagavad Gita* already contained this message in its emphasis on socially engaged action or the path of karma yoga. "First of all, our young men must be strong. Religion will come afterwards," he began. "You will understand the Gita better with your biceps, your muscles a little stronger. You will understand the mighty genius and the mighty strength of Krishna better with a little of strong blood in you."[32] Vivekananda approvingly quotes Krishna's admonition to Arjuna, as a directive to young India: "Yield not to unmanliness, o Partha" (2.3). During Vivekananda's cross-cultural career as a public speaker, the *Gita* conveyed differing messages to different audiences, depending on the swami's sense of the needs of his American or Indian listeners.

Through Vivekananda's direction (no doubt influenced by the organizational practices of the Christian missionaries he otherwise disdained), the *Gita*'s this-worldly orientation took institutional form in India in the Ramakrishna Mission. The monastic followers of Ramakrishna would devote themselves not to meditation or devotional worship but instead to alleviating poverty and suffering by establishing hospitals and schools as well as organizing relief during famines and natural disasters.

Vivekananda died suddenly in 1902, at age thirty-nine. The organizations that he initiated in the United States and India, however, continued his work. Moreover, his successful passage from India to the West set an itinerary for other Hindu swamis and gurus to journey westward. From Vivekananda's first remarks in Chicago, the *Bhagavad Gita* served as a key reference for his lectures, but the swami never completed a sustained translation or commentary on the work. Other swamis of the Ramakrishna Order serving in Vedanta Centers in the United States did publish translations and commentaries, including swamis Abhedananda, Nikhilananda, and Prabhavananda. Many other Hindu gurus have utilized the *Gita* as the fulcrum in their efforts to translate Hindu teachings—of widely differing types—for American and Western audiences. Some like Swami Parthasarathy present the *Bhagavad Gita* as a philosophical argument for strict Advaita nondualism. Others like Bhaktivedanta portray the *Gita* as a fervent devotional poem. Still others represent it as a foundational work for the physical and mental practices of integral yoga, transcendental meditation, or many other varieties of yoga. They have exercised a powerful say in how these audiences receive and understand the *Gita* as a still-living Hindu scripture.

Through his passage, Vivekananda brought some of the "far-darting beams of the spirit" that Whitman celebrated from a land of an elder religion to the New World. (Vivekananda in turn praised Whitman as "the sannyasin of America."[33]) At the same time, his success in the United States and effort to establish a more activist form of Hinduism in India, using Krishna's presentation of karma yoga, contributed to a vital conversation in colonial India. The debate was political and cultural as much as religious: how to create a new, more assertive national ethos as part of the growing movement to gain independence from British control. The *Bhagavad Gita* would play a major role in this discussion.

Krishna, the *Gita*, and the Indian Nation

CHAPTER 4

Sanjaya said: "Wherever Krishna the lord of yoga and Arjuna the archer are, there too will be good fortune, victory, prosperity, and firm good conduct. That's what I believe."
—*Bhagavad Gita 18.78*

In 1926, Swami Shraddhananda proposed a new kind of institution for promulgating the *Gita*. "The first step which I propose," he wrote, "is to build one Hindu Rashtra mandir [temple of the Hindu nation] at least in every city and important town, with a compound which could contain an audience of 25 thousands and a hall in which Katha from Bhagavad Gita, the Upanishads and the great epics of Ramayana and Mahabharat could be daily recited." He suggested that a "life-like map of Mother-Bharat" be placed in proximity in each of these new temples, "so that every child of the Matri-Bhumi [motherland] may daily bow before the Mother and renew his pledge to restore her to the ancient pinnacle of glory from which she has fallen!"[1]

Shraddhananda was a leader of the Arya Samaj, a large Hindu reformist group, and took an active role in the movement for Indian independence from British colonial rule. During Gandhi's first nationwide satyagraha campaign against the Rowlatt Act in 1919, Shraddhananda led the mobilization in Delhi. As his plan for temples of the Hindu nation indicates, he envisioned the *Bhagavad Gita* playing a key role in creating victory and prosperity for the nation of India, symbolized in the form of Mother Bharat. No longer just a matter of facilitating liberation of individual souls through the paths of knowledge or devotion, as the medieval commentators had interpreted it, Krishna's yoga in the *Gita* would now be redeployed for the liberation of an entire nation, restoring it to an "ancient pinnacle of glory." It would do so, in Shraddhananda's proposal, through an institution for the mass recitation of Krishna's words, reaching audiences far greater than ever before in the *Gita*'s life.

Shraddhananda had another agenda here as well. In the 1920s, the swami became active in the Hindu Sangathan (Hindu solidarity) movement. He had come to see other religions in India, primarily Islam and Christianity, as posing a threat to the Hindu majority and Indian nationhood. He feared that conversions of lower-class Hindus by Muslims and Christians would lead to the disintegration of the ancient class system, a bulwark of Indian social structure. The Muslims had their large congregational spaces, the Jami Masjids, and their single holy text, the Quran. Shouldn't the Hindus construct similar places for mass assembly, he reasoned, and select for themselves a shared sacred "bible"? For Shraddhananda, the *Bhagavad Gita* would be mobilized to help unify and consolidate a specifically Hindu nation in the face of internal religious enemies to the nation-building project.

Swami Shraddhananda's vision for nationwide assembly halls for *Gita* recitation did not come to fruition on the scale that he proposed, although a number of "Gita Temples" and "Gita Halls" were constructed in the following decades.[2] Still, the *Bhagavad Gita* did gain a vastly wider distribution than ever before in early twentieth-century India through numerous vernacular translations and mass publication of inexpensive editions by publishers such as the aptly named Gita Press of Gorakhpur. The *Gita* came to play a crucial role in the thinking and discourse of leaders of the Indian independence movement, including Lala Lajpat Rai, Aurobindo Ghose, Bal

FIGURE 7. Shrimad Bhagavad Gita Mandir, Mathura, built by Raja Baladeva Das Ji Birla, 1946.
Photograph by the author.

Gangadhar Tilak, and Gandhi. Yet as Shraddhananda's double agenda indicates, the promotion of the *Gita* as a national text could quickly slip into a more sectarian or "communal" agenda. In an anticolonial movement that aspired to be cohesive and unifying on a national scale, the *Gita* and other Hindu symbols could be seen as divisive, since they excluded non-Hindu communities. Or in another direction, the relevance of the *Gita* could be projected beyond Hinduism and India to embrace all humanity as a universal spiritual work.

The dramatic growth in readership and interpretive interest in the *Bhagavad Gita* in early twentieth-century India raises several questions. Why did so many Indian leaders and activists adopt the *Gita* as a central work in their efforts? How did they interpret Krishna's teachings in light of their situations and aims? And where did the *Gita* lead them? If the presence of Krishna and Arjuna assures good fortune and victory, as Sanjaya promises, just what are the good fortune and victory they could deliver?

Quest for a Historical Krishna

Krishna was still very much alive in late nineteenth-century India. Writing in the 1880s of his native Bengal, the patriotic novelist and essayist Bankim Chandra Chatterjee observed:

> In Bangal, the worship of Krsna is virtually pervasive. Krsna's temples in village after village, Krsna's worship in house after house, Krsna's festivals in almost every

month, Krsna-plays in festival after festival, songs of Krsna from voice after voice, the name of Krsna on all lips. The garments of some carry Krsna's name; the bodies of others are imprinted with Krsna's name. None will start his journey without taking Krsna's name; none will begin a letter or commence study without writing Krsna's name; the beggar does not ask for alms without uttering "Hail Radha-Krsna!"[3]

In other regions throughout the subcontinent, the devotional traditions surrounding the cowherd god Krishna flourished as well, in homes and temples, festivals and dances, and songs.

Western scholars, meanwhile, had come to regard Krishna as a mythical character. Krishna was a composite of several different legends. To British eyes, Krishna's lack of historicity reflected the woeful lack of historical consciousness among Indians. As Mill put it with his usual asperity, ancient Indian literature contained "not a single production to which the historical character belongs." In India, he goes on, "the actions of men and those of deities are mixed together, in a set of legends, more absurd and extravagant, more transcending the bounds of nature and of reason, less grateful to the imagination and taste of a cultivated and rational people," than those of any other civilization in the world.[4]

Even as a mythical being, Krishna was found wanting. This supposed deity was associated with frivolity, self-indulgence, sensuality, and immoral conduct. His amorous conduct with the Gopis, described in the *Bhagavata Purana* and many later poems, was seen as particularly reprehensible. Those who devoted themselves to such a god were also judged harshly. Writing of the Pushtimarg community of Krishna devotees, the eminent British Indologist Monier Monier-Williams observed that they interpreted the attachment of Krishna and the Gopis "in a gross and material sense." As a result, he continued, "their devotion to Krishna has degenerated into the most corrupt practices and their whole system has become rotten to the core."[5] For British colonials, Krishna stood as a symptom of what was wrong with India.

For educated Indians of the emerging nationalist movement, Krishna's bad reputation was a problem. The cowherd Krishna of the *Bhagavata* and later devotional tradition cut an unworthy figure, they agreed, but the teachings that the adult Krishna set forth in the *Bhagavad Gita* offered great promise. Could they perhaps make Krishna a more reputable model for the needs of the time rather than a remnant of the medieval past? The solution would be to reconstruct the character of Krishna on firmer historical grounds, much as European writers like Ernest Renan were doing with the character of Jesus. This task was taken up by several leading nationalist writers and politicians in the late nineteenth and early twentieth centuries, starting with Chatterjee in his *Krishna-Charitra*, followed by Lajpat Rai's *Yogiraj Shri Krishna* and other similar works. The result was a recalibration of Krishna's personality. His early life among the cowherds of Vraja was radically amended or jettisoned, while his grown-up role in the *Mahabharata* as well as, especially, his battlefield dialogue with Arjuna in the *Gita* were promoted. No longer a self-indulgent child or seductive adolescent, the historical Krishna should be seen, as Lajpat Rai put it, as "a great teacher, a great warrior, and a man of great learning."[6]

Lawyer, journalist, educational reformer, relief worker, and political leader, Lajpat Rai wrote a series of short biographies of "Great Men of the World" in the 1890s, addressed to the youths of India. Quoting Thomas Carlyle, Lajpat Rai stated that great men are like sparks of the great fire that provides light to the world and brings happiness to humanity. He hoped that these sparks would kindle national idealism in young people. He began with Giuseppe Mazzini, followed by Giuseppe Garibaldi. Indian nationalists were keenly interested in the success of the Italian risorgimento, for it too had needed to overcome internal divisions and foreign oppression in order to consolidate a unified, independent nation-state. After the Italians, Lajpat Rai turned to Indian worthies. He wrote on Shivaji, the seventeenth-century Marathi warrior and ruler, and Dayananda Saraswati, founder of the Arya Samaj. Finally he took on Krishna, in *Yogiraj Shri Krishna*, published in 1900.

Lajpat Rai admits at the outset that Krishna has been portrayed in an unflattering light. In their "excessive enthusiasm," poets have done Krishna a grave injustice, creating all kinds of misconceptions about him in the minds of the Indian people. "They have so pierced him with the arrows of their petty and vulgar imaginations," Lajpat Rai says of the devotional poets, "that his personality has totally changed and as a result most of the Aryans considering him impure and sensual have developed an aversion to him."[7] How can one reconcile the frivolous depiction of the cowherd Krishna, tempting lover of the Gopis, with the dignified teacher of the *Bhagavad Gita*?

To write a historical biography of an ancient figure like Krishna, there is of course a serious problem of sources. One must cull facts, says Lajpat Rai, from the imaginary and hyperbolic accounts of poets. He therefore starts with a discussion of the available sources and his own historical method. Lajpat Rai assumes that earlier sources are more trustworthy than later ones, which over time have been corrupted by poetic fancy. Puranas like the *Bhagavata*, he acknowledges, cannot be treated as historical sources, even though they contain the most extensive accounts of Krishna's life. The Puranas have fundamentally altered Krishna's personality, in Lajpat Rai's view. The *Mahabharata* is a more ancient composition, he observes, and thus closer in time to the life of Krishna. Even here, Lajpat Rai must admit that the epic poem is a composite work that includes later additions. The most reliable basis for a historical biography of Krishna is contained in the oldest strata of the *Mahabharata*.

How old is that oldest strata? Lajpat Rai acknowledges that it is difficult to determine the exact date of the *Mahabharata* war, since there are no other historical sources from that ancient period. He does cite one estimate, based on astronomical details mentioned in the text, that place it at least 3,426 years back, at 1520 BCE. Whether or not we accept that calculation, Lajpat Rai states that we can safely date the Bharata war and core composition describing it to a period earlier than the Upanishads. Some scholars, he says, contend that the entire *Mahabharata* story is fictive, and that its heroes like Krishna and the Pandavas are imaginary literary creations. To counter this, Lajpat Rai cites the many references to these figures throughout Sanskrit literature, thereby proving Krishna's real historical existence. Was Krishna an incarnation of God? Lajpat Rai believes that Krishna never made any such claim, nor did anyone else during his lifetime give him that title. The incarnation theory is a "creative projection" added later to enhance Krishna's prestige. Krishna's doubleness as a human and divine figure is poetic hyperbole.

In Lajpat Rai's estimation, Krishna was a human warrior and ruler who lived in ancient northern India during the early Vedic period, fought in the great war narrated in the *Mahabharata*, and presented teachings to his friend Arjuna on the battlefield that formed the core message of the *Bhagavad Gita*. Later Indian tradition turned Krishna into an incarnation of God, supplemented his original teachings in the *Gita* with later topics, and appended a frivolous youth onto this admirable figure.

After this preamble, Lajpat Rai can proceed to tell the life of Krishna as a "model human being." His life, in Lajpat Rai's telling, exemplifies Krishna's primary teachings in the *Bhagavad Gita*. These hold valuable lessons relevant to the present. Lajpat Rai identifies two dangerous tendencies among contemporary youths in colonial India. The first is Western materialism. The atheism of Europe, observes Lajpat Rai, has seduced the minds of many youths, weaning them from the fundamental truths of Hinduism and leaving them open to the Western way of life. "According to them the aim of life is nothing but to eat delicious food, wear fashionable clothes, travel in luxury vehicles, and live in comfort."[8] The second danger is the opposite of this: the Indic tradition of world renunciation. Some Indian youths think only of spiritual development and hold all worldly pleasures as contemptible.

The life and teachings of Krishna present a better alternative to both dangers. Krishna urges Arjuna to do his duty and fight, not to renounce or indulge himself. "According to Krishna's teachings," Lajpat Rai concludes, "it is the duty of a Kshatriya, until he earns the right to be called a Brahmin, to fight against his enemies, and if in order to uphold religion, righteousness and truth, he has to take up arms and risk his life he should not hesitate to do so."[9] What Lajpat Rai has in mind is that Indian youths should commit themselves to opposing British colonial rule, even if that involves risking their lives—as he did.

Varieties of Karma Yoga

In 1907, Lajpat Rai was arrested for leading widespread agrarian agitations in the Punjab region and deported without trial to Mandalay Fort in Burma. While in prison, he wrote a lengthy article on the "Message of the *Bhagwad Gita*," published in the *Modern Review*.[10] In his interpretive essay, Lajpat Rai stresses that

Krishna's primary purpose in the *Gita* is to persuade Arjuna to fight. All else is secondary to the activist message. Past commentators on the *Gita*, Lajpat Rai observes, have often neglected this central agenda in Krishna's discourse, and instead emphasized the paths of knowledge, devotion, or some other philosophical doctrine. Dharma or duty should be the supreme law of one's life, and once one recognizes that duty, no consideration of self-interest, love, or mercy should distract one from it. As such, Krishna above all advocates the path of karma yoga. This has clear present-day political implications, according to Lajpat Rai. Quoting Sanjaya's concluding statement about the beneficial presence of Krishna and Arjuna, he continues, "A nation's prosperity and success depend upon wisdom like that of Krishna and bravery like that of Arjuna." As in the *Mahabharata*, a crisis looms in early twentieth-century India. "If ever any nation stood in need of a message like that of Krishna, it is the India of today."[11] Despite his own incarceration in Burma, Lajpat Rai ends on a hopeful note. If his fellow Indians are able to heed this message from the *Gita*, India's future is just as assured as the victory of Arjuna over the Kaurava forces at Kurukshetra.

Lajpat Rai was not the only one to enlist the *Bhagavad Gita* in the cause of Indian independence. The *Gita* was particularly significant for those who, like Lajpat Rai, sought a more active, confrontational, "masculine" response to British colonial rule. They too valued Krishna's emphasis on selfless duty-based worldly action and viewed the path of karma yoga as his most important teaching. Yet among these activist interpreters of the *Gita* there were profound differences. They range from the young revolutionaries of the Anushilan Samiti and Yugantar, through the so-called Extremists like Aurobindo and Tilak active in the Indian National Congress, to Hindu nationalists like Shraddhananda and K. S. Hedgewar, founder of the Rashtriya Svayamsevak Sangh (RSS).

To gain entry to the inner circle of the Anushilan Samiti (Self-Culture Association), a police surveillance report of 1909 stated, an initiation was required. Lying flat on a human skeleton, holding a revolver in one hand and a copy of the *Bhagavad Gita* in the other, the initiate had to recite the group's oath.[12] The Anushilan Samiti formed a cadre-based revolutionary network centered in Bengal in the early part of the twentieth century. Other similar groups operated largely underground in Maharashtra, Punjab, and other parts of India. Samiti members were convinced that insurrectionary violence against the British was the best path for gaining independence for India, and sought to catalyze this uprising through propaganda and terrorist actions. They trained themselves in the use of *lathi*, sword, and other weapons, and celebrated the virtues of manly strength to counter the British stereotype of Indian effeminacy.

Two types of literature circulated within the Anushilan Samiti. One was practical: how-to works on bomb making and other military techniques. The other was ideological: works like the *Bhagavad Gita*, intended to provide a rationale and stimulus for the group's revolutionary activities. Krishna's advice to Arjuna was constantly quoted in the revolutionary books and newspapers.[13] The young revolutionaries saw the fullest religious foundation for their efforts in the Kshatriya dharma of the *Gita*, Krishna's persuasive urging of Arjuna to fight in a righteous battle, and the text's emphasis on selfless devotion to a greater cause. The revolver in one hand and *Gita* in the other at initiation symbolized the practical and ideological limbs of their revolt.

Lying on a corpse symbolized the willingness to die in the cause of freedom. The young revolutionary Khudiram Bose was inspired by the speeches of Ghose and his readings of the *Bhagavad Gita* to join Yugantar (New Era), the underground group led by Aurobindo's brother Barinchandra Ghose. In 1908, Khudiram and his confederate Prafulla Chaki carried out a bomb attack on the carriage of District Judge D. H. Kingsford. They selected the judge as target because he had been responsible for bringing cases against activist newspapers like Aurobindo's *Bande Mataram* (I bow to the Mother). Kingsford was not in the carriage at the time, but the bomb did kill the wife and daughter of a local British barrister. Khudiram was apprehended and sentenced to death by hanging. At the gallows, it was reported, the eighteen-year-old youth died cheerful and smiling, holding a copy of the *Bhagavad Gita*, with the final words, "Bande Mataram." Many would celebrate him as one of the first martyrs of the Indian struggle for independence.

Clandestine groups like the Anushilan Samiti and Yugantar did not leave extensive written records on matters like *Gita*-interpretation. But Aurobindo's early writings illustrate how the *Bhagavad Gita* fit within the developing ethos of the independence movement in the early twentieth century.[14] Aurobindo was an early critic of the elitist orientation and moderate reformism of the Indian National Congress in the 1890s, and soon affiliated himself with others, such as Lajpat Rai and Tilak, who advocated Indian independence as the first and highest priority. Within Congress circles they were called the Extremists. Aurobindo operated aboveground as a journalist and spokesperson within Congress, but also worked covertly in support of underground groups like the Anushilan Samiti and Yugantar.

Similar to Lajpat Rai, Aurobindo's initial reading of the *Gita* focuses on the central importance of action. He criticizes those Vedanta commentators of the past such as Shankara who had highlighted the value of renunciation. Writing in his aptly named weekly journals *Bande Mataram* and *Karmayogin* (which featured an image of Krishna and Arjuna in their chariot on the cover), Aurobindo proclaims karma yoga as the means by which India could gain independence from Britain and fulfill itself as a nation. To achieve this righteous end, violence is an acceptable means, much as Krishna explained to Arjuna.

Aurobindo gives a strong spiritual valence to this nation. Drawing both from European nationalists like Mazzini and Indian theistic traditions, he envisions Indian nationhood as a kind of divine force. "Nationalism is a religion that has come from God," he emphasizes, and if there is one "over-mastering idea" to Indian nationalism, he continues, it is the conviction "that there is a great Power at work to help India, and that we are doing what it bids us."[15] With the divinization of the nation, Aurobindo integrates the devotional dimension of Krishna's teachings into his understanding of karma yoga. Just as Krishna directs Arjuna to act as his instrument in the great battle at Kurukshetra, Aurobindo urges his audience of activists to see themselves as agents of a divine Power in their battle for an independent Indian nation.

In contrast to the *Gita*, however, Aurobindo does not identify this overarching Power as Krishna. Instead, it is a Goddess. Within Indian nationalist circles the nation was widely seen as a great Mother Goddess, called Kali, Durga, Bhavani, or most commonly Bharat Mata (Mother India). This newcomer to the Indian pantheon first took shape in an influential novel by Chatterjee, *Anandamath* (1880). Chatterjee's novel also contributed the song "Bande Mataram," which became the anthem of the early Indian freedom fighters. Aurobindo added to her growing cult with a 1905 pamphlet, "Bhawani Mandir" (Temple of the Goddess), and the title of his first journal, *Bande Mataram*. The cult of the nation-goddess continued in Shraddhananda's proposal in the 1920s to have the Mother India goddess installed in every temple of the Hindu nation, so that her children could daily bow before her. Reversing the older bhakti paradigm of Krishna and the Gopis, in this new gendered (and nonerotic) nationalist devotionalism, the masculine activists would render their services as devoted sons on behalf of the feminine Mother India.[16]

Around 1905, at the height of his journalistic and political activities, Aurobindo began to experiment with the yogic disciplines of breath control and meditation. He did so not as a renouncer but rather as an engaged worldly activist who needed the strength and wisdom that these practices might provide. He hoped, in other words, to become a "person of settled wisdom," a sthitaprajna, as Krishna describes it. But the results of his practices, along with the repercussions of his covert political involvements and Krishna's apparent intervention, would lead him away from leadership in the nationalist movement on to a new path and into an expanded understanding of the *Bhagavad Gita*. We will return to Aurobindo's second career later in this chapter.

Aurobindo's senior colleague in the extremist wing of the Congress, Tilak, a journalist, also devoted concentrated attention to the *Bhagavad Gita* as a key ideological work for the Indian struggle. Tilak was arrested in 1908 for articles in his newspaper that British officials claimed celebrated Khudiram and his partner for their bomb attack at Muzaffarpur. The British contended that those articles might incite more terrorist acts. Tilak was convicted and sentenced to six years of hard labor in Mandalay prison, Burma. While in jail, he composed a substantial new commentary on the *Gita*, which he termed a *rahasya* or "hidden doctrine," as if he were disclosing a previously concealed meaning in the ancient work. His *Srimad Bhagavadgita Rahasya*, published in the Marathi language in 1915, was quickly translated into Hindi, Gujarati, Bengali, Kannada, Telugu, and Tamil, and became one of the two most influential of all Indian nationalist interpretations of the *Gita*.[17]

Like Aurobindo, Tilak argues adamantly for an activist or "energist" reading of Krishna's teachings, against the older "escapist" Vedantic interpretations of Shankara, Ramanuja, and Madhva. In Tilak's view, interpretation of a religious work like the *Gita* must be historically situated. While he admits that Shankara's knowledge-oriented reading of the text may have been justified during the "Age of Renunication" in which Shankara lived, the present

FIGURE 8. *B. G. Tilak Composing His Gita Rahasya in Mandalay Prison*, detail from mural painting of Tilak's life by Gopal Damodar Deuskar at Tilak Smarak Mandir, Pune.
Author's photograph. Tilak is depicted in jail, with Krishna and Arjuna appearing before him as he writes.

period is an "Age of Karma," and the *Gita* must be interpreted in accord with the needs of the age. As with Aurobindo, Tilak accepts that this action might include violence, provided it is carried out without any desire to reap the fruit of the violent deeds. But herein lies a quandary of dharma.

In the *Gita*, Arjuna's duty to exercise violence in battle is grounded first of all on his dharma as a Kshatriya, a member of the warrior class. In classical India, this class enjoyed a monopoly on legitimate violence in order to preserve the social order and protect proper political authority. Tilak himself was a Brahmin by birth and clearly recognized that India could not rely solely on its remaining Kshatriya groups to carry out a struggle for freedom from British colonial control. As he saw it, the pressing need was to enlist all Indians in this battle. Tilak's historical interpretation offers a solution to the problem of a class-based dharma in the *Gita*. In a class society where public duties were clearly ordered and separated, as in the time of the *Mahabharata*, Tilak acknowledges, it was appropriate to call on Kshatriyas in times of war. In the present situation of foreign occupation, though, the duty of public service should fall on all citizens. In effect, British colonialism turns all Indian citizens into potential Kshatriyas.

The practical question for Tilak and other activist leaders was how to mobilize larger masses on behalf of the struggle for an independent Indian nation. Throughout his career, Tilak experimented with ways to enlist the Indian population in this effort. In the 1890s, he transformed a local Maharashtrian festival for the god Ganesha into a large public celebration, and he established a new festival to honor Shivaji. Since British officials were reluctant to interfere in Indian religious affairs, these annual public events provided an opportunity to bring together people of all classes, both urban and rural. They also enabled Tilak and other activists to convey covert political messages at these mass gatherings. In Tilak's tactical thinking, Hinduism was the surest magnet to attract the Indian masses. It had a liability as well. Ganesha was an indisputably Hindu deity, and Shivaji was most famous for his militant resistance to the authority of the Mughals, an Islamic regime. So while the festivals might bring the Hindu population together, they could alienate other religious communities, especially the Muslim population. The Indian National Congress was committed to an Indian nation that included all communities, and Hindu-centered mobilization strategies threatened to fracture this solidarity.

Similar drawbacks lay in the new cult of the nation-goddess Bharat Mata and promotion of the *Bhagavad Gita* to bible-like status. This became apparent in the 1920s with the emergence of Hindu nationalism in several new incarnations: the Hindu Sangathan movement, the revived Hindu Mahasabha, and the RSS. The fundamental question raised by these new groups concerned the identity of the putative Indian nation. Would India be defined as a territorial nation, a geographic entity inclusive of all persons and communities within its borders, as the Indian National Congress asserted? Or would

India be defined as an ethnic nation whose essential nature resided in its Hindu-ness, as the Hindu nationalist groups advocated? Would Bharat Mata be the goddess of a geographic nation or a religious one? In the early 1920s, Shraddhananda came to the conclusion that the ethnic or religious definition should prevail. His proposal for the mass recitation of the *Gita* and homage to the Mother India goddess in temples of the Hindu nation signals how the *Bhagavad Gita* could be allied with Hindu nationalist projects.

Another karma yogin devoted to the Hindu nation was Hedgewar, who established the RSS in 1925.[18] As a youth in Maharashtra, Hedgewar had avidly read Tilak's newspaper writings and found inspiration in the heroism of Shivaji. He joined the Anushilan Samiti for several years during his time in Calcutta for medical study. Returning to Maharashtra in 1916, Hedgewar made the decision to renounce both marriage and medical practice to dedicate himself unequivocally to the freedom movement. In 1920 he worked tirelessly in Gandhi's noncooperation campaign, and was sent to prison for his efforts. Hedgewar occupied his time in jail with spinning and reading the *Bhagavad Gita*, the book of choice among imprisoned Indian freedom fighters. Released in 1922, he gradually withdrew from the Indian National Congress. Hedgewar came to believe that only Hinduism could motivate the population to achieve independence and reform society. Unfortunately, as he saw it, the Hindu community was weak and divided. To remedy that affliction, he organized the RSS.

The primary aim of the RSS was to build strength and character among Hindu males, and the model for that character-building enterprise grew out of Hedgewar's reading of the *Gita*. Each person has a divinely implanted dharma, a set of duties and responsibilities. To act in accord with that dharma contributes to the well-being of society; to act contrary to dharma is egocentric behavior disruptive of the social order. Krishna's teaching of *nishkama karma* (action without desire) is crucial in directing individuals to perform their social obligations with detachment and humility. Beginning with young boys, Hedgewar designed RSS training to engage them in both physical and moral cultivation that would make them effective karma yogins.

For Hedgewar, the path of karma yoga is best when combined with the discipline of devotion. Ideally the RSS *svayamsevak* (voluntary servant) should devote himself to the "living God" that is the Hindu nation, represented as the feminine Divine Mother. At the highest levels of cultivation, the RSS karma yogin would remove all layers of individual ego identity and merge his own ego with that of the nation. This can be seen as a nationalist adaptation of Krishna's devotional ideal. In Hedgewar's understanding, threats against the Mother come not only from external British colonial rulers but also from within. Indian Muslims and Christians who promulgate values contrary to the dominant Hindu ethos, and likewise those Westernized Indian elites who would reform Hindu society along European lines (whether that be capitalism, socialism, or communism), all pose insidious dangers. Devotion to Mother

India therefore requires action directed against both external colonialism and internal others. The Divine Mother needs all the help she can get.

Not all Indian nationalists looked to the *Bhagavad Gita* for moral support, of course. One prominent critic was the lawyer and Dalit spokeperson Bhimrao Ramji Ambedkar. In his writings on the *Gita*, Ambedkar insisted that it be seen as a historical work, composed at a certain time, and he criticized those who sought to give it a universal significance. In its own time, he argued, the *Bhagavad Gita* was a counterrevolutionary defense of Vedic practices and the hierarchical class system favored by Brahmins, aimed against the powerful critique of Buddhism. Krishna cleverly appropriated many Buddhist tenets in order to make his counterargument, says Ambedkar, but at its core Krishna's teaching aimed to supply a divine foundation for the brahmanic social order, and it supported genocide over the Buddhist principle of nonviolence. Ambedkar proposed that Buddhism offers a superior ethical foundation for Indian nationhood.[19]

Gandhi's Nonviolent *Gita*

Of all the Indian nationalist readers of the *Bhagavad Gita*, none was more dedicated to it than Gandhi, the Mahatma. He referred to it as a "spiritual reference book," "dictionary of daily reference," "book of home remedies," "wish-granting cow," and "mother," and returned to it over and over again throughout his life for clarification and nurturance.

Gandhi first read the *Gita* around 1888 or 1889, when studying law in London, in the company of some theosophical friends. Together they read the poetic translation of Arnold, *The Song Celestial*, alongside Arnold's popular retelling of the life of the Buddha Shakyamuni, *The Light of Asia*, and the Christian Bible. "My young mind tried to unify the teachings of the *Gita*, *The Light of Asia*, and the Sermon on the Mount," Gandhi later remembered, pointing to the open-ended and experimental way that he sought spiritual and practical instruction from any available religious source.[20] Along with his theosophist friends, he approached the *Gita* not as a specifically Hindu or Indian text but rather as a possible revelation or source of Truth.

During his public career, Gandhi made the *Bhagavad Gita* a constant point of reference in his talks and writings. He considered the work his "infallible guide to conduct." When he returned from South Africa to India in 1915, Gandhi established an ashram at Sabarmati, and made recitation of the *Gita* a central part of the daily morning and evening prayer sessions, along with hymns and prayers from other religious traditions. Imprisoned in the early 1920s, Gandhi carefully read Tilak's *Gita Rahasya* and other translations, and began to compile his own *Gitakosh*, a glossary of terms from the work. In 1926 Gandhi presented a series of talks on the *Gita* at his ashram, amounting to a sustained commentary on the work, and in 1929 made his own Gujarati translation.

FIGURE 9. Mahatma Gandhi during evening prayer at Sabarmati
Ashram, Ahmedabad, 1930, photograph by Samaldas Gandhi.
Reproduction courtesy GandhiServe, Berlin.

Also in 1929 he composed an introduction to the translation, "Anasaktiyoga" (the discipline of nonattached
action), which is his most succinct interpretive statement on the *Gita*. The introduction and translation
were released on March 12, 1930, the day that Gandhi
began his salt satyagraha. Again in prison from 1930 to
1932, Gandhi wrote a series of letters to the ashram, giving a simplified chapter-by-chapter summary of Krishna's teachings for those who found his earlier commentary difficult to comprehend. His last recorded
discussion of the *Gita* took place with the American
writer Vincent Sheean in January 1948, three days before his assassination.

In writing on the *Bhagavad Gita*, Gandhi does not
claim any scholarly credentials for himself. His authority

lies rather in his attempt to govern his life according to its precepts. "At the back of my reading," he writes in his "Anasaktiyoga," "there is the claim of an endeavor to enforce the meaning in my own conduct for an unbroken period of forty years."[21] Beyond this personal dimension, Gandhi's interpretation of the *Gita* is a deeply political act. Writing in the 1920s, Gandhi faces several challenges. Like other activists, he views karma yoga as the most relevant teaching of the *Gita*. But in light of his own commitment to nonviolence (*ahimsa*) and his desire to make this a fundamental principle of the Indian independence movement, he needs to counter those like Tilak as well as the revolutionaries who employ Krishna's teachings to justify the use of violence in a righteous cause. At the same time, he seeks to separate the *Gita* from the more Hinduist claims on the text, like those of the Hindu Sangathan or the RSS.

The *Mahabharata* is not history, Gandhi asserts. Instead, it is a work that treats "religious and ethical questions." Gandhi is indifferent to the question of Krishna's historical existence. Krishna is "perfection and right knowledge personified," he states, but the portrait is imaginary.[22] Krishna may have lived, but the idea of him as a divine incarnation is a later invention.

Gandhi's disinterest in historical veracity lays the groundwork for an allegorical reading of the epic and the *Gita*. Kurukshetra, in Gandhi's internalist reading, is within each of us. The epic battle is a struggle between dharma and its opposite, between the forces of good and evil. "Pandavas and Kauravas, that is, divine and demoniacal impulses, were fighting in this body, and God was watching the fight from a distance," Gandhi explains. "Please do not believe that this is the history of a battle which took place on a little field near Hastinapur. The war is still going on."[23] As a nonhistorical moral allegory, the *Mahabharata* and its *Bhagavad Gita* have permanent value.

The objective on this interior battlefield is "to become like unto God," to attain "self-realization." The singular path to accomplishing this, Gandhi declares, is through renunciation of the fruits of action. This principle is "the unmistakable teaching of the *Gita*." Along with Krishna and the other activists, Gandhi emphasizes that this kind of renunciation can be carried out in the midst of worldly activities. There is no line of demarcation between worldly pursuits and salvation. Like Lajpat Rai and Tilak, Gandhi criticizes those who follow paths of renunciation or devotion to the exclusion of worldly duties. "The popular notion of *bhakti*," he remarks, "is soft-heartedness, telling beads and the like, and disdaining to do even a loving service, lest the telling of beads, etc., might be interrupted." This brand of religious devotionalism gets in the way of work. Such a devotee, Gandhi goes on, "leaves the rosary only for eating, drinking, and the like, never for grinding corn or nursing patients."[24] For Gandhi, by contrast, there is no higher ideal than that of the *sthita-prajna*, who utilizes the yogic disciplines of self-control to carry out social duties—whether those be grinding corn, nursing patients, or working for the independence of India—without attachment. This is the true yogi. At

Gandhi's ashram, the section of the *Gita* describing the sthitaprajna would be recited at every evening prayer session as a recurrent reminder.

What about the fact that Krishna successfully urges Arjuna to engage in a battle of unquestionable violence? How does Gandhi account for this central theme of the *Bhagavad Gita*? First of all, he points out that the *Mahabharata* is not a glorification of physical warfare but rather a proof of its futility. The victors shed tears of sorrow and repentance, and are left with nothing but a legacy of miseries. More specifically, when Krishna tells Arjuna to "fight," he means simply that Arjuna should do what he regards as his duty. Since every action requires a choice, doing one's duty always requires an inner struggle. The internal battle to overcome our own tendencies to act according to self-interested desires and instead base our actions on disinterested responsibility is the perpetual fight that Krishna urges on us all.

Gandhi engages Tilak's interpretation more directly over one particular passage. In Gandhi's translation it goes: "In whatever way men resort to Me, even so do I render to them. In every way, O Partha, the path men follow is mine" (4.11). Tilak cited this verse to prove that the *Gita* upholds the principle of "tit for tat," or retributive violence. We should act toward others as they do to us. The aggressive violence of British occupation, Tilak had argued, may legitimately be met with violent resistance by freedom fighters. Gandhi counters that the verse cannot be interpreted in this way. We cannot justify retributive violence. The verse lays down God's law, Gandhi observes, and not a directive for human interaction. Krishna will "worship a person as the latter worships Him." As Gandhi sees it, the message of the verse is "we reap as we sow."[25]

Krishna does not explicitly endorse the principle of nonviolence in the *Gita*, Gandhi admits. Nevertheless, nonviolence is a corollary of Krishna's primary teaching—namely, nonattachment to the fruits of action. Any action that cannot be performed without attachment is taboo, and this means that murder, lying, dissoluteness, and the like are disallowed. Although the *Gita* was not written to justify nonviolence, Krishna takes it for granted. To reinforce this point, Gandhi cites his own experience. Perfect renunciation such as Krishna advocates is not possible without perfect observance of nonviolence.

The principle of nonattachment applies even to the righteous work of the freedom struggle. The danger with nationalist thinking, according to Gandhi , is that it may lead to the adoption of "bad means," which Gandhi terms *duragraha*. "If we are attached to our goal of winning liberty, we shall not hesitate to adopt bad means." Gandhi refers here to all those nationalists who justify acts of vilification or violence by citing noble goals, such as victory, prosperity, and good fortune. By contrast, Krishna recommends that we should not be attached even to a good cause. "Only then will our means remain pure and our actions, too."[26]

Gandhi ends his disquisition on the *Bhagavad Gita* by stressing the value of Krishna's teachings for the hard work of discipline that he urges on himself, members of his ashram, and all who read his words. He reiterates his conviction that the *Gita* is a work of universal ethics, not the possession of a particular national or religious community. "This is a work which persons belonging to all faiths can read. It does not favor any sectarian point of view. It teaches nothing but pure ethics."[27] The *Gita* may be, as Gandhi puts it, a "deity of the mind," but it is not an exclusive "Hindu Bible."

Gandhi's nonviolent and nonsectarian reading of the *Bhagavad Gita* would prove enormously influential in India, disseminated through his newspapers, publications, and translations into all the vernacular languages. At the time, many Indians fit Gandhi himself into the theological framework of the *Gita*. Just as Krishna says that he incarnates himself in age after age, whenever dharma is threatened, perhaps Gandhi was the avatara of this age.[28]

Not all Indians shared Gandhi's approach to the text, of course, or judged him with such reverence. Ironically, Gandhi's assassin also saw himself as a *Gita*-style karma yogin. In January 1948, after Indian independence and the catastrophic communal violence surrounding the partition of the subcontinent, Gandhi began to hold daily public prayer sessions in Birla House, Delhi, reciting passages from the *Gita* and Quran along with religious works from other traditions. On the evening of January 30, Nathuram Godse interrupted Gandhi at the prayer grounds with two bullets fired at point-blank range.

As a youth, Godse had first become politically active in Gandhi's civil disobedience campaigns of 1929 and 1930, but soon became disillusioned. Gandhi's policies were too pro-Muslim, he decided. Godse joined the RSS in 1932.

FIGURE 10. *Mahatma Gandhi*, chromolithograph,
artist unknown.
Published by Subhash Picture Publishers. Author's
collection. Gandhi's characteristic iconography
includes a copy of the *Gita Updesha*.

Here too the restless militant was frustrated by the group's
inactivity, and later withdrew to form a more radical
group, the Hindu Rashtra Dal. He believed that Gandhian
nonviolence was useless as a political weapon and was
leading to an "emasculation" of the Hindu community.
Godse instead praised past revolutionaries like Aurobindo
and Khudiram, and held that it was "a religious and moral

duty to resist and if possible overcome foreign occupation by force."[29] For Godse, the dismemberment of Mother India through the partition and ensuing violence against its Hindu population were the final insults. He held Gandhi's politics of appeasement responsible and decided it was his duty to rid the nation of its enemy.

Two days before his execution, Godse wrote a final letter to his parents in which he affiliated himself with Krishna and his teachings. Krishna killed Shishupala, Godse noted, yet did so not on the battlefield but rather on "holy sacrificial ground." No doubt Godse had in mind his own action at a place of prayer. "Lord Krishna, in war and otherwise, killed many a self-opinionated and influential persons for the betterment of the world, and even in the *Gita* He has time and again counseled Arjun to kill his near and dear ones and ultimately persuaded him to do so."[30] So too Godse had come to believe that Krishna's directives to Arjuna applied to his own assassination of the influential Gandhi for the world's betterment. On the morning of his execution, in the tradition of Khudiram, Godse carried a copy of the *Bhagavad Gita* and uttered as his final words, "Bande Mataram."

Aurobindo's Universalizing Vision

Though Godse cited Aurobindo's early teachings to justify his action, Aurobindo himself had long ago taken a different course. To take up Aurobindo's second career, we need to return to the time of Khudiram's unsuccessful but consequential bomb attack on Justice Kingsford in 1908. After the bombing police quickly swooped in on known subversives, including Barinchandra and others in the Yugantar cadre. They found bomb materials, weapons, and incriminating documents, including many copies of the *Bhagavad Gita*. The police also arrested Aurobindo on suspicion that he was "ringleader" of the whole revolutionary network. The alleged conspirators were charged with "waging war on the king"—a treasonous offense punishable by death. The ensuing Alipore bomb trial was a complicated, lengthy, and contentious legal event, widely reported in newspapers throughout India. Barinchandra was eventually convicted and sentenced to death, but his penalty was later commuted to life imprisonment. As for Aurobindo, the prosecution could not establish any clear incriminating evidence linking him to the crime. He was acquitted and released after a year in jail.

Aurobindo's life was transformed by his time in prison. Shortly after he was released, Aurobindo described his experiences in a remarkable impromptu speech. First put into solitary confinement, Aurobindo relates, he had tried to meditate, but initially found it difficult. He soon received a copy of the *Bhagavad Gita*, however, and then was able to progress in his efforts.

> I was not only able to understand intellectually but to realize what Sri Krishna demanded of Arjuna and what He demands of those who aspire to do His work, to be free from repulsion and desire, to do

work for Him without the demand for fruit, to renounce self-will and become a passive and faithful instrument in His hands, to have an equal heart for
high and low, friend and opponent, success and failure, yet not to do His work negligently.

Applying Krishna's teachings to his own situation enabled Aurobindo to gain mastery over the impatience
and despair that had hindered him. With this, Aurobindo says, he began to realize the "central truth of
the Hindu religion."[31]

Prison officials compassionately allowed him to begin
taking brief walks outside his cell, and while he was doing
so, Aurobindo reports, "God's strength" entered into him.

> I looked at the jail that secluded me from men and it
> was no longer by its high walls that I was imprisoned;
> no, it was Vasudeva [Krishna] who surrounded me. I
> walked under the branches of the tree in front of my
> cell but it was not the tree, I knew it was Vasudeva, it
> was Sri Krishna whom I saw standing there and hold-
> ing over me his shade. I looked at the bars of my cell,
> the very grating that did duty for a door and again I
> saw Vasudeva. It was Narayana [Krishna] who was
> guarding and standing sentry over me.[32]

Like Arjuna granted divine vision in the *Gita*, Aurobindo received God's grace and gained a visual realization of Krishna's all-encompassing presence. And as
with Arjuna's vision on a field of battle, this manifestation of Krishna's divine nature responded to Aurobindo's
own problematic situation—his incarceration.

The vision enabled Aurobindo to see his fellow prisoners in a divine light. "I looked at the prisoners in the jail, the thieves, the murderers, the swindlers, and as I looked at them I saw Vasudeva, it was Narayana whom I found in these darkened souls and misused bodies." Later, brought into the courtroom, Aurobindo was able to envision Krishna pervading the place: the magistrate sitting on the bench was Krishna, and the prosecuting counsel was also Krishna. Aurobindo reports that he heard the voice of Krishna reassuring him, saying,

> I am in all men and I overrule their actions and their words. My protection is still with you and you shall not fear. This case which is brought against you, leave it in my hand. It is not for you. It was not for the trial that I brought you here but for something else. The case itself is only a means of my work and nothing more.[33]

Similar to Arjuna at Kurukshetra, Aurobindo at Alipore came to see himself as an instrument in Krishna's greater plan.

What was that "something else" that Krishna had in mind for Aurobindo? In his speech Aurobindo explains that in prison, he gained a deeper realization about his work. Up to then Aurobindo had been involved in political work aimed at "uplifting the nation," but while in jail he recognized the deep truth of the Hindu religion. Now he reports that the Hindu religion, which he terms the "eternal dharma," has a destiny. It is to go forth "to do its work among the nations. . . . That which we call the

Hindu religion is really the eternal religion, because it is the universal religion which embraces all others."[34] The struggle to liberate the Indian nation from colonial control forms only one part of this greater global spiritual mission. Aurobindo has received a call to devote himself to Krishna's larger project.

Free from jail, Aurobindo continued to give speeches and edit the weekly *Karmayogin*, for which he wrote most of the articles. In 1910, in the wake of another revolutionary assassination of a British officer, the government cracked down on all insurgents. Officials initiated a sedition charge against Aurobindo for one of his articles. Meanwhile, Aurobindo received what he called a "sudden command from above" to get out of Calcutta and take refuge in a nearby French territory. From there he made a secretive escape to Pondicherry, another French territory in the southern part of the subcontinent, free from the reach of British law.

Aurobindo spent the remaining forty years of his life in Pondicherry. Although he never renounced his earlier political work and never ruled out a possible return to British India, he lived in Pondicherry as a virtual renouncer, turning his attention to other matters he now considered more important. He saw this shift as an expansion of the scope of his work. Previously he had been concerned with "the service and liberation of the country," but henceforth he viewed his aim as "world-wide in its bearing and concerned with the whole future of humanity."[35] To this end he deepened his meditative practices, and described in voluminous detail his inner experiences as well as his vision of integral yoga and spiritual evolution on a global scale. Gradually an ashram took shape in Pondicherry around Aurobindo.

The *Bhagavad Gita* continued to play a significant role in Aurobindo's new work. Starting in 1916, he wrote two series of interpretive essays exploring themes in the *Gita*, later collected in book form as *Essays on the Gita*. In the first essay Aurobindo sets out his approach. He starts by pointing to the doubleness of the *Gita*, as of any lasting religious scripture.

> First of all, there is undoubtedly a Truth one and eternal which we are seeking, from which all other truth derives, by the light of which all other truth finds its right place, explanation and relation to the scheme of knowledge. . . . Secondly, this Truth, though it is one and eternal, expresses itself in Time and through the mind of man; therefore every Scripture must necessarily contain two elements, one temporary, perishable, belonging to the ideas of the period and country in which it was produced, the other eternal and imperishable and applicable in all ages and countries.[36]

Aurobindo declares himself uninterested in the historicist approach, which deals in the temporary and perishable. He wishes to seek in the *Gita* the permanent living truths applicable to "the spiritual needs of our present-day humanity." Likewise, he is disdainful toward the "polemist commentators" of the medieval period who sought to confine the *Gita* within a

FIGURE 11. Aurobindo Ghose in Pondicherry, ca. 1915, photograph.
Reproduction permission courtesy Sri Aurobindo Ashram Trust, Pondicherry.

narrow ontological consistency. The *Gita* is not itself a systematic work, Aurobindo observes, but rather a synthesizing one. In it there is "a wide, undulating, encircling movement of ideas which is the manifestation of a vast synthetic mind and a rich synthetic experience."[37] Seen in this way, the *Gita* is not a "weapon" for dialectical warfare but instead a "gate" that opens out into a world of spiritual truth and experience.

Here the agenda of the *Gita* in the time of its composition matches the need of the twentieth century, as Aurobindo sees it. The author of the *Gita* reconciled and unified the many contending religious viewpoints and practices in the India of its time. Similarly, Aurobindo argues, "we on the coming day stand at the head of a new age of development which must lead to a new and larger synthesis." The *Gita* presents itself as a point of departure by which Aurobindo can begin to articulate that new synthesis. Not a historical work of the past, not a philosophically consistent doctrinal text, and not anymore a Hindu or Indian scripture, the *Bhagavad Gita* carries an "essential and living message" that all humanity needs for its own spiritual evolution in the new global age.[38]

While Aurobindo set forth his universalizing interpretation in Pondicherry, the *Bhagavad Gita* continued its prolific life in India. It was not simply a work of the Hindu past. All readers viewed it as relevant to contemporary life, but they saw its relevance in different ways. The work took on multiple identities, almost as if Krishna had adopted several incarnations simultaneously in response to diverse needs. And each interpretive identity would have its own legacy.

For Hindu nationalists from the RSS through Godse to the Hindutva campaigns of the 1980s and 1990s, the *Gita* would serve as a representative icon of a unitary Hindu heritage to be defended against threat from enemies outside and within the nation. Krishna's teachings could provide a warrant for even violent actions intended to protect the dharma embodied in the Hindu population.

For the Indian activists allied with Gandhi, the teachings of the *Bhagavad Gita* would define and reinforce the disciplined and dispassionate practices of nonviolent karma yoga at the center of the struggle for Indian independence. Thanks to its role in Gandhi's thinking, the *Gita* would be passed on to many other activists engaged in struggles against oppression around the world up to the present day.

For Aurobindo and his disciples, the *Gita* would serve as a crucial starting point for a new spiritual synthesis extending to all humanity. Along with Vivekananda, Aurobindo would be a paradigm for those Indian gurus, increasingly numerous in the West from the 1960s on, who would adopt ancient Hindu texts and teachings for new modern audiences in India and throughout the world. More than any other Hindu text, the *Bhagavad Gita* would be the vehicle for these new teachings.

Modern *Gitas*: Translations

> Krishna said: "The one who shows me the highest devo-
> tion and shares the highest mystery [of these teachings]
> with my devotees will reach me, no doubt about it. No
> other person does me greater service than this. No one in
> the world is dearer to me."
>
> —*Bhagavad Gita 18.68–69*

At the conclusion of his discourse, Krishna commends to
Arjuna the great value in disseminating the teachings
contained in the *Bhagavad Gita*. Reading this passage in
the early twentieth century, Jayadayal Goyandka heard
Krishna giving him direction for his own life. Goyandka
was a member of the entrepreneurial Marwari community, and he had decided that the great service he could
provide would be in the publishing business. He established the Gita Press in 1923, and began to publish inexpensive editions of the *Bhagavad Gita* with Hindi translation, making the work widely available throughout
northern India. Later the press brought out translations
in fourteen major Indian vernacular languages. Its Web

site currently lists one 123 different *Gita* publications, including translations and commentaries. It was his dream, Goyandka later recalled "to see the Bhagavad Gita and other scriptures made available in each and every household of the land, just as the British made tea and tobacco available everywhere throughout the country."[1] The Gita Press reports that it has now sold 71 million copies of the *Gita* in Hindi, Gujarati, Telugu, Oriya, and other vernacular Indian languages as well as Sanskrit.

As with every great religious work of antiquity, the continuing and expanding life of the *Bhagavad Gita* depends on its engaging new audiences in languages other than its original. After the Christian Bible, the *Gita* is certainly one of the most frequently translated works in the religious literature of the world. In the most thorough bibliographic study of this text, covering the years up to 1982, Winand Callewaert and Shilanand Hemraj found 1,412 published translations of the *Gita* in 34 Indian languages. Around the world they identified 1,891 translations in 75 languages.[2] In English alone, they were able to locate 273 published translations of the work in the two centuries since Wilkins first rendered it into English in 1785. And new translations have appeared every year in the three decades since their study. The *Bhagavad Gita* has reincarnated itself in English-language publications well over 300 times.

One might add to this list, as indirect translations, novelized reworkings of the *Gita* theme and teachings. Among these, the earliest is Chatterjee's 1884 Bengali novel, *Debi Chaudhurani*, in which Krishna's teachings are imaginatively put into practice in a modern setting by a female protagonist. More recently, Krishna has been shifted from charioteer to African American golf caddy in Steven Pressfield's *The Legend of Bagger Vance* (1995), set in Georgia during the Depression.

The *Gita*'s New Clothes

Krishna compares the process of a soul's reincarnation to a person changing clothes: "Just as a person might take off old clothes and put on other new ones, so the soul abandons an old body and enters into other new ones" (2.22). Translations of the *Gita* also reembody the Sanskrit source in new forms, each one striving to retain some essential aspect of the original. But unlike a soul reincarnating in one new body, a new translation does not require the death of old ones. It simply adds to the expansive life of the original text. We live in a world containing many diverse embodiments of the *Bhagavad Gita*, a large closetful of *Gita*s.

Each translation results from a series of choices. These choices reflect the translator's own premises, aims, and conception of what that work most essentially is. In a valuable study of *Gita* translations in English, Gerald Larson speaks of the "strategic decisions" every translator must make. He analyzes these along four axes: the stylistic pedagogical, interpretive, and motivational continua.[3] Does the translator seek to maintain primarily the stylistic character of the Sanskrit original or to produce a literary rendering in appropriate English? What kind of audience does the translator envision for the work? Does the translator consider the task as rendering the meaning of the work in its time of composition or as it might take on new significance in contemporary times? What personal motivations or subjective reasons does the translator bring to the task of translating the *Gita*? Along with the skill that any translator brings to the task of navigating between Sanskrit and English, these strategic decisions together will help determine the shape of the *Gita*'s new English clothes.

There are also choices involved in the textual accompaniments that surround a translation in the body of a publication, or the "paratext" in Gerard Genette's productive phrase.[4] Does the book also contain interspersed commentary? Or parallel Sanskrit text? Does it have footnotes, and what issues do these notes address? Does it have an introduction? What topics are addressed there? How do these materials relate the *Bhagavad Gita* intertextually to other religious and literary works? As Genette reminds us, these "threshold" materials extend the work itself, mediating between the primary text and its public audience, guiding readers toward and within the translation.

In this chapter I consider four exemplary modern translations of the *Bhagavad Gita* into English, all from the period since World War II and Indian independence. They were selected from the three-hundred-plus possibilities to highlight distinct approaches to the work. In each case, the translation reflects fundamental commitments and choices of the translators: an accomplished Indological scholar, a poet who specializes in world religious literature, a prominent guru from a Vaishnava devotional lineage, and a distinguished Indian philosopher grounded in the Advaita Vedanta tradition. My aim here is not to evaluate translations according to standards of fidelity or felicity but instead to observe the differing ways each publication extends the continuing life of the *Bhagavad Gita* within the modern world.

A Scholar's *Gita*

"In the course of translating the *Mahabharata*," writes Van Buitenen, "I was bound to reach the point where, in that last moment of stillness before the battle, Arjuna shrinks away from its abomination, and Krsna, his friend and charioteer, persuades him of its necessity."[5] An erudite Dutch Indologist and distinguished professor of Sanskrit at the University of Chicago, Van Buitenen took on the monumental task of translating the entire *Mahabharata* single-handedly. Working his way diligently through the great epic, he had already completed its first five books before he reached the *Bhagavad Gita*, early in the sixth book or *Bhishma-parvan*. This prolonged journey through the *Mahabharata* to reach the *Gita* was formative for the commitments and strategic choices behind Van Buitenen's scholarly translation, titled *The Bhagavad Gita in the Mahabharata* (1981).

As an Indologist, Van Buitenen is committed to a contextual and historical reading of the *Gita*. He argues persuasively in his introduction that the *Gita* was "a creation of the *Mahabharata* itself," rather than an independent work that somehow "wandered into" the epic at some later date. To make his case, he summarizes the plot to highlight Arjuna's dilemma, which he sees as a tension fundamental to the *Mahabharata* as a whole. He also includes eight chapters preceding the usual eighteen of the *Bhagavad Gita* proper as well as the chapter after it to demonstrate the "subtle narrative weaving" that binds the *Gita* into the *Mahabharata*.[6]

In his introduction, Van Buitenen also locates the *Gita* as part of the social and religious discourse of classical India. In its own historical time of composition, he argues, the *Gita* addressed vital contemporary ethical, theological, and metaphysical issues. The work adapted concepts from other Indic schools of thought such as Mimamsa, Vedanta, Samkhya, Yoga, and Buddhism, and it put forward innovative new ideas carefully disguised as old ones. Van Buitenen uses his introduction to sketch the historical background necessary for the reader to view the *Gita* in its classical milieu. While he is certainly aware that the *Gita* has led a rich continuing life since that time, Van Buitenen's emphasis is decidedly on the *Gita* in the time of its Indian composition.

Van Buitenen chooses to render the *Bhagavad Gita* primarily in prose, as he does for most of the *Mahabharata*. The great majority of the epic was composed in the *shloka* form, a flexible verse form consisting in four

unrhymed lines of eight syllables each, with some syllables required to be long or short. Indian poets found this
verse form particularly amenable for narrative composition, and the simple rhythmic pattern suited it well for
oral recitation. An enormous amount of classical and medieval Sanskrit was written in shloka form. By rendering
the epic shloka in prose rather than English verse form,
and running the verses together into paragraphs rather
than enshrining each one separately, Van Buitenen hopes
to convey the conversational quality of the original, "the
friendly and at times intimate tone and the directness of
language" characteristic of the work.[7] Many readers,
however, will not find Van Buitenen's translation particularly friendly. It retains numerous Sanskrit terms and
stays close to the intricate technical arguments that
Krishna often advances, instead of paraphrasing or introducing extrinsic concepts. In keeping with the scholarly
approach, this publication includes the Sanskrit text, in
Roman transliteration, on opposing pages to facilitate
easy reference to the original for those acquainted with
the original language.

In his historicist approach, Van Buitenen continues a
venerable lineage in Western Indological scholarship devoted to the *Bhagavad Gita*. Appearing first with Wilkins
and other British Orientalists of late eighteenth-century
Calcutta, and taking institutional form in nineteenth-
century Germany with philologists and scholars like the
brothers Schlegel, the *Gita* has been maintained in many
university settings in India, Europe, and North America
by professors of Sanskrit like Van Buitenen. Their central

task is to reconstruct the history and culture of ancient and classical India, especially as it was transmitted in Sanskrit texts. From Wilkins's time on, the *Gita* has provided a particularly valuable and challenging window into that historical world, resulting in a steady stream of erudite translations and scholarly studies. Other noteworthy translations in the Indological lineage prior to Van Buitenen include those of Telang (1882) and Edgerton (1944). For a persistent reader, Van Buitenen's translation and introduction offers the closest available approximation of the *Bhagavad Gita* in its original context.

A Poet's *Gita*

What if one takes the *Bhagavad Gita* not just as a historical artifact of classical India but also as a profound religious poem addressing "some of the most important truths of human existence"? This is the point of departure for Stephen Mitchell's *Bhagavad Gita: A New Translation* (2000). "The Gita is usually thought of as a great philosophical poem," he writes in his introduction. "It is that, of course. It is also an instruction manual for spiritual practice and a guide to peace of heart. But essentially it is, as its title implies, a love song to God."[8] For Mitchell, the task of the translator differs dramatically from that of a textual historian like Van Buitenen. The resulting translation and publication is bound to look quite different in diction, style, and content.

Mitchell is a talented poet and prolific translator of religious literature from around the world. He has taken on the poetry of Rainer Maria Rilke and Yehude Amichai. Mitchell has rendered numerous ancient classics, including the Book of Job, the *Tao Te Ching*, selected portions from Genesis and Psalms in the Hebrew Bible, and the *Epic of Gilgamesh*. More recently he has added the *Iliad* to this impressive corpus of translations. In translating the *Gita*, Mitchell makes no claim to fluent knowledge of Sanskrit or any expertise in ancient Indian religious thought. Scholarly readers may criticize Mitchell for this, but it does not appear to bother him. There are, he observes, plenty of English *Gita*s from which to work.

The main problem, as Mitchell sees it, lies in finding a suitable verse form in English to render the Sanskrit shloka. He seeks a form that has the "dignity of formal verse," yet is also "free and supple enough to sound like natural speech."[9] His choice is a loose trimeter quatrain. Each shloka is treated as a separate unit of four lines, three stressed syllables per line. By isolating individual shlokas (as most translators do), Mitchell may lose some of the conversational or discursive style that Van Buitenen hopes to capture. But each verse can stand on its own, like pearls in a necklace, as a potential starting point for reflection and meditation. Respecting the integrity of the poem, Mitchell does not impose any of his own commentary, nor does he include annotations to the translation.

If Van Buitenen guides the reader toward a world of classical India, filled with debating proponents of various religious persuasions, Mitchell's introduction encourages the reader to locate the *Gita* in a timeless circle of sages. Emerson and Thoreau, Lao Tzu, Chinese Zen masters, a Sufi sheikh, Jesus, the Hebrew prophets, Gandhi, and Ramana Maharshi—all are invoked to inhabit this gathering of agreeable religious teachers and "spiritually mature human beings" from all times and places. Like these other teachers, says Mitchell, the *Gita* speaks directly to a fundamental question: How should we live? Krishna does not set out just to change Arjuna's life but rather to transform all of us. It is an inward transformation, Mitchell emphasizes. He imagines the *Gita* speaking to Emerson and Thoreau as a "kinsman, an elder brother," revealing to them truths they already knew, albeit imperfectly. So too we all possess, somewhere within us, the wisdom that Krishna has to teach. A poem like the *Gita* can remind us of this latent understanding and bring these truths into consciousness.

Mitchell's translation is not the first poetic *Gita* in English. The legacy of literary translations began with Arnold's charming 1885 blank-verse rendering, which made such an impact a few years later on the young Gandhi. Another distinguished literary rendering is the translation coauthored by California-based Vedanta Society teacher Swami Prabhavananda and British novelist Christopher Isherwood, published in 1944. Seeking to avoid the pitfalls of Indological translations with their "obscurity and archaic un-English locutions," Isherwood tried to match the different types of discourse he found in the *Gita* with a mixture of English styles, both prose and verse, instead of sticking with a single verse form.[10] Others have attempted to combine a scholarly attention to the Sanskrit original with a poetic rendering in English, including the recent versions by Barbara S. Miller (1986) and Laurie Patton (2006).

By placing the *Bhagavad Gita* among a select circle of mystical writings, Mitchell continues another lineage. I call this the "perennialist" line, following Huxley's *The Perennial Philosophy* (1945).[11] The successful British novelist moved to the United States in 1937, and toured the country lecturing on pacifism. During World War II, he intensively studied mystical religious works, especially Indian ones. Huxley collected passages from the works of saints, prophets, and sages from all traditions that, he argued, conveyed a single shared mystical worldview encompassing metaphysics, psychology, and ethics. He called this the "Highest Common Factor." As Huxley explained to Henry Miller, he sought to present the doctrine "taught by every master of the spiritual life for the last three thousand years—a doctrine of which the modern world has chosen to be ignorant, preferring radios and four-motored bombers and salvation-through-organization, with the catastrophic consequences that we see all around us."[12] Writing in California during the cataclysm of the Second World War, he came to see this mystical religion as the sole hope for the world's survival.

Of all the works he synthesized, Huxley stated that Krishna's battlefield teachings at Kurukshetra offered the most systematic scriptural statement of the perennial philosophy. Mitchell's California at the beginning of the twenty-first century appears to be a more serene place, and he sees personal transformation rather than the salvation of world civilization as the *Gita's* primary agenda. But Huxley and Mitchell, and many others in California and elsewhere, have shared the conviction that this work of classical India addresses issues and provides guidance that is universal, timeless, and pertinent to all humans.

A Devotee's *Gita*

For Bhaktivedanta, also known as Swami Prabhupada, the essential fact about the *Bhagavad Gita* is its speaker. The *Gita* contains the words of Krishna, and Krishna is the "Supreme Personality of the Godhead." Just as Arjuna accepts Krishna as the divine Absolute during their conversation, so Swami Prabhupada accepts Krishna. In his view, all readers of his translation should do so, too. The teachings of the *Gita* are infallible because the original teacher is perfect. This places stern demands on the translator. Prabhupada sees his task as passing on the "mission" or presenting the "will" of Krishna. Other translations, he writes, are not authoritative because the translators have expressed their own opinions in them. By contrast, Prabhupada's translation claims to present the *Bhagavad-gita As It Is*.

Prabhupada was a vigorous seventy-year-old Bengali Vaishnava renouncer when he arrived by steamship in the United States in 1965. He had been initiated three decades earlier into the Gaudiya Vaishnava community, which traced itself back to the sixteenth-century Bengali devotional saint Chaitanya. In the 1930s, Prabhupada's direct guru, Bhaktisiddhanta Sarasvati, had urged Prabhupada to write in English and spread Krishna Consciousness to the West. Accordingly, Prabhupada spent many years diligently working on an English translation of the *Bhagavata Purana*, which the Gaudiya tradition considered the preeminent scripture. When he finally gained passage to the United States, the renouncer traveled with just forty rupees and almost no personal possessions except his precious India-published translation of the first canto of the *Bhagavata*.

Prabhupada soon began chanting the names of Krishna and conducting *Gita* classes on New York's Lower East Side. He attracted a group of curious and eager followers there, and shortly thereafter, also in the Haight-Ashbury neighborhood of San Francisco, both centers of the 1960s' youth counterculture. From this grew the International Society for Krishna Consciousness (ISKCON), one of the most successful and certainly most visible of all the new Hindu groups established in the United States during the 1960s.[13]

As he began teaching to new acolytes, however, Prabhupada quickly recognized that the *Bhagavad Gita* was a better starting point than the *Bhagavata* for conveying the essentials of Krishna Consciousness. In 1966–67, he worked devotedly on a new translation of the *Gita* that could be published and distributed in the United States. It was published first by Macmillan in an abridged version in 1968, and in 1972 an unabridged version came out.

This was the first translation of the *Gita* I owned, given to me by Chicago followers of Prabhupada in 1972.

To present the *Gita* "as it is" to a new Western audience, Prabhupada adopts an Indian pedagogical mode of presentation. Each individual verse is given first in Sanskrit Devanagari script and then in Roman transliteration. Every word of the verse is glossed, and then Prabhupada gives his translation of the verse, followed by his own commentary, often quite lengthy, intended to unpack the religious significance or "purport" of the verse. Prabhupada indicates little interest in the poetry of the composition, and his presentation makes it difficult to read the *Gita* apart from the apparatus surrounding it. That is consonant with Prabhupada's conception of the text and of his own purpose. The *Gita* presents "Vedic knowledge," and he wishes to convey and explain this universal truth fully to his Western followers.

The *Bhagavad Gita*, as Prabhupada sees it, intends to transform a reader into a devotee of Krishna. This is an urgent task, for we live in the ever-deteriorating conditions of the Kali-yuga, the age of decline. "The purpose of the *Bhagavad-gita*," he remarks, "is to deliver mankind from the nescience of material existence."[14] The *Gita* is best understood by any reader who can identify with Arjuna. Just as Arjuna was confused on the battlefield, all sensitive humans are confronted with anxieties caused by living in a material world. Arjuna was already a friend of Krishna, and by hearing Krishna's teachings he came to accept him as the highest Absolute. So too the modern reader should accept Krishna, at least theoretically, as the

Supreme Divinity, Prabhupada proposes, for the teachings of the *Gita* to make sense. The same salvation offered to Arjuna is available to everyone through the transmitted words of the *Bhagavad Gita*, which teaches Krishna's Supreme Personality and the appropriate path of devotional service to him. For Prabhupada and his lineage, the supremacy of Krishna and discipline of bhakti are unequivocally the *Gita*'s central themes. Other paths in the *Gita* appear only as steps toward bhakti.

Many Indian gurus coming to the United States to promulgate various forms of Hinduism have adopted the *Bhagavad Gita* as a key text to present their teachings. First were the teachers of the Vedanta Centers established by Swami Vivekananda, such as Swami Abhedananda and Swami Nikhilananda. The translation by Prabhavananda and Isherwood also falls within this lineage. Among the 1960s' generation of Hindu gurus, Maharishi Mahesh Yogi (founder of Transcendental Meditation) published a partial translation, *On the Bhagavad-Gita*, in 1966, and Swami Satchidananda (founder of Integral Yoga) published *The Living Gita*. Prabhupada's work was the first English translation of the *Gita* to supply an authentic interpretation from an Indian devotional tradition. And thanks to the indefatigable efforts of his ISKCON followers, the *Bhagavad-gita As It Is* has become by far the most widely distributed of all English *Gita* translations. The Bhaktivedanta Book Trust estimates that twenty-three million copies of Prabhupada's translation have been sold, including the English original and secondary translations into fifty-six other languages.[15]

A Philosopher's *Gita*

"Every scripture has two sides," writes Sarvepalli Radhakrishnan, "one temporary and perishable, belonging to the ideas of the people of the period and the country in which it is produced, and the other eternal and imperishable, and applicable to all ages and countries."[16] Radhakrishnan recognizes the doubleness of the *Bhagavad Gita*, a scripture that is both historical and abiding. While he acknowledges and respects the historical conditions of its composition, this modern Vedanta philosopher takes as his primary task in translating the *Gita* to offer "a restatement of the truths of eternity in the accents of our time." Writing in the years immediately after World War II and the partition of British India into Pakistan and India, Radhakrishnan believes that the world's pressing need is for the "reconciliation of mankind." The *Gita*, he holds, is particularly well suited to this purpose.

Radhakrishnan embodied doubleness throughout his own life. As a child from a pious South Indian Brahmin family sent to Christian missionary schools, he became interested in comparative philosophy and religious ethics as a way to reconcile the tension he experienced between Hindu devotion and Christian doctrine. He became a leading advocate for the philosophical viewpoint of Advaita Vedanta, whose greatest exponent was the lifelong renouncer Shankara. But unlike that ascetic, Radhakrishnan led an active life engaged in worldly affairs, including stints as ambassador, vice president, and president of the republic of India. He held academic positions in both colonial India and imperial Britain, where he was a Spalding Professor of Eastern Religion and Ethics at Oxford. In the midst of this doubleness, Radhakrishnan sought reconciliation. The dominant thrust of his philosophical work was to find commonality between the Indian and European traditions in a shared idealism. More broadly still, he hoped to find accord between religious and spiritual values and the dominant scientific and materialist worldview of the twentieth century.

This emphasis on reconciliation runs through Radhakrishnan's understanding of the *Bhagavad Gita* as well. The main inspiration of the *Gita*, he maintains, came from the Upanishads, but its purpose was to refine and draw together the various currents of the thought and practice of its time into an "organic unity." Moreover, the *Gita*'s historical unification transcends its own day. The author of the *Gita*, says Radhakrishnan, "reconciles the different systems in vogue and gives us a comprehensive eirenicon which is not local and temporary but is for all time and all men."[17] The modern Vedantin Radhakrishnan agrees with key parts of Shankara's medieval interpretation: nondualism, the centrality of "spiritual experience," and the superiority of the path of knowledge. In contrast to Shankara, though, Radhakrishnan also highlights the value of ethical action in the world. He takes seriously Krishna's charge to Arjuna to carry out his duties, as part of the *Gita*'s perennial message.

As an Indian philosopher writing for a general and international audience, Radhakrishnan chooses a commentarial mode of presentation for his translation. Individual verses appear first in Sanskrit transliteration and then in prose translation, followed by brief commentary. Radhakrishnan's prose does not aspire to elegance; his aim is to convey the meaning of each verse directly. In the commentary, Radhakrishnan cites various Vedic and classical Indian works as well as the principal Vedanta commentators. These references ground the translation in its Indic tradition. Radhakrishnan occasionally goes further afield, referring to parallel ideas in works of poets (Emerson and Wordsworth), Christian writers (Saint Augustine and Thomas Aquinas), and Western philosophers (Plato, Plotinus, and Spinoza). By doing so, Radhakrishnan lifts the *Gita* out of its own cultural world into the single shared world of humanity to which he believes it ultimately belongs.

Radhakrishnan's own legacy is complex. His primary philosophical debt is to the Vedanta tradition and particularly the nondualist school of Shankara. Coming of age in the first half of the twentieth century, Radhakrishnan followed Vivekananda and Aurobindo as key figures in the modern restatement of the Vedanta perspective, sometimes called "neo-Vedanta." Radhakrishnan met with Gandhi in 1947 at Birla House in Delhi and received permission to dedicate his translation of the *Bhagavad Gita* to him. Following Gandhi, Radhakrishnan emphasizes the vital importance of ethical action in the world—not always part of the Vedanta outlook. Straddling the transition from colonial India to independence in 1947, he discovered a new opportunity to address a postcolonial world just emerging from the horrors of World War II. The *Gita* could do double duty. Radhakrishnan's translation is a work that speaks to and for the newly independent Indian nation-state. Like Radhakrishnan himself, the classical *Gita* is an ambassador representing India on the global stage. At the same time he views the *Gita* as a work that may assist humanity in the "great movement toward integration" occurring in the twentieth century, from "national societies" into the "world whole."[18]

"The Shatterer of Worlds"

To illustrate these four distinct approaches to the task of translating the *Bhagavad Gita* for modern audiences, let us look at how each translator renders the same passage. I select two verses with unmistakable resonance for modern society.

On July 16, 1945, at the dawning of the atomic age, J. Robert Oppenheimer watched the first human-controlled atomic explosion at Los Alamos, New Mexico, from a bunker twenty miles away. As director of the Manhattan Project, Oppenheimer was responsible for overseeing the creation of the bomb, which the project called "Trinity." He was a brilliant professional physicist, and also a gifted amateur student of Sanskrit. As he observed the awesome detonation of Trinity, Oppenheimer later recalled, passages from the *Bhagavad Gita* sprang to his mind.

If the radiance of a thousand suns
Were to burst at once into the sky,
That would be like the splendor
    Of the Mighty One . . .
I am become Death
The shatterer of worlds.[19]

These occur in the *Gita* during Arjuna's vision of
Krishna's all-encompassing form. The second excerpt
is part of Krishna's own explanation to the awestruck
warrior. Since the warriors on the battlefield are already destroyed by his own divine will, Krishna goes
on to urge Arjuna to act as his instrument in the upcoming war. Oppenheimer undoubtedly shared Arjuna's anxiety and dread as he watched the atomic con-
flagration, and he later came to portray his own role in
the worldwide conflict as an instrument of a higher
authority, much as Arjuna did.

This passage is certainly a dramatic one, but it is relatively simple and devoid of technical terms. Yet one can
readily discern, by juxtaposing Van Buitenen's and Mitchell's treatment, significant differences in translational approach and presentation.

Since this passage departs from the usual shloka meter,
Van Buitenen shifts from prose to verse format, but his
scholarly approach shows through.

The Lord said:
I am Time grown old to destroy the world,
Embarked on the course of world annihilation:
Except for yourself none of these will survive

Of these warriors arrayed in opposite armies.
Therefore raise yourself now and reap rice fame,
Rule the plentiful realm by defeating your foes!
I myself have doomed them ages ago:
Be merely my hand in this, Left-handed Archer.[20]

This approaches a literal translation, sticking as closely to the Sanskrit word order as is feasible here. Yet there is little effort, along the stylistic continuum, to create a literary rendering in English verse. The Sanskrit original contains a consistent eleven syllables in each quarter, and a set pattern of long and short syllables. Van Buitenen makes no discernible attempt to create a parallel patterning in the target language. For him, certainly, the meaning of the passage must come foremost.

Mitchell takes greater care to create a pleasing English rhythm in his verse, but also shortens the passage.

The Blessed Lord said:
I am death, shatterer of worlds,
annihilating all things.
With or without you, these warriors
in their facing armies will die.
Therefore stand up; win glory;
conquer the enemy; rule.
Already I have struck them down;
you are just my instrument, Arjuna.[21]

Mitchell aims at the central message here and conveys it succinctly. A comparison of the two renderings will show, however, the cultural detail that Mitchell must leave out to arrive at his more forceful treatment: the old age of Time, the specific exclusion of Arjuna from death's grip, the plenitude of the kingdom that Arjuna may rule after victory, and more. Such historical accuracy is less important, in Mitchell's approach, than creating a version that will speak directly to his modern English-speaking audience.

Swami Prabhupada brings a different motivation to the task. The goal is to demonstrate Krishna's divinity and explicate his message within a Gaudiya Vaishnava perspective. Prabhupada chooses prose, interspersed with his "Purport." "The Supreme Personality of Godhead said: Time I am, the great destroyer of the worlds, and I have come here to destroy all people. With the exception of you [the Pandavas], all the soldiers here on both sides will be slain." He expands the "blessed lord" of Mitchell to "Supreme Personality of Godhead," the fundamental principle of his religious orientation. Krishna's own words here appear less dramatic and more conversational. After the verse, Prabhupada reminds the reader of Arjuna's initial reluctance to fight and observes that the widespread death to come is part of Krishna's plan. "Time is destruction," Prabhupada continues, "and all manifestations are to be vanquished by the desire of the Supreme Lord. That is the law of nature." Following his two paragraph commentary, the translator goes on to the next verse. "Therefore get up. Prepare to fight and win glory. Conquer your enemies and enjoy a flourishing kingdom. They are already put to death by my arrangement, and you, O Savyasaci, can be but an instrument in the fight."

This passage leads Prabhupada to emphasize the comprehensiveness of Krishna's design. "The whole world is moving according to the plan of the Supreme Personality of Godhead." It is thus salutary to understand this divine plan rather than lord it over material nature. "If one is in full Krsna consciousness and if his life is devoted to His transcendental service," Prabhupada assures his readers, "he is perfect."[22]

Like Prabhupada, Radhakrishnan adopts the Indic format of verse and commentary, but his commentary leads in a different direction. He interjects a heading to the passage, "God as the Judge," then gives his prose translation. "The *Blessed Lord* said: Time am I, world-destroying, grown mature, engaged here in subduing the world. Even without thee (thy action), all the warriors standing arrayed in the opposing armies shall cease to be." It seems that Radhakrishnan wishes to soften Krishna's dramatic statement with Time only "subduing" and not "destroying" the world, and his quaint Victorian "thee" and "thy" are bound to distance a modern reader. But his commentary pushes toward a universal theology. The Krishna who speaks here is identified as God, and his message is likened to Christian theological concepts. "There is an impersonal fate, what the Christians call Providence, a general cosmic necessity, *moira*, which is an expression of a side of God's nature and so can be regarded as the will of His sovereign personality, which pursues its own unrecognizable aims." From here, Radhakrishnan moves to the next verse, in which Arjuna says, "Therefore arise thou and gain glory. Conquering the foes, enjoy a prosperous kingdom, By me alone are they slain already. Be thou merely the occasion, O Savyas-acin."[23] This verse leads Radhakrishnan to a lengthy discussion of human agency in light of the divine will, in which citations from the Bible—Job, Luke, and Paul—serve to familiarize and underscore Krishna's brash commands. In his commentarial exposition, Radhakrishnan here situates Krishna in a theological dialogue with the Judeo-Christian tradition, aiming at a broader understanding in which the *Bhagavad Gita* will take its place as one expression of a universal human philosophy encompassing East and West.

What is the best English-language translation of the *Bhagavad Gita*? That will of course depend on the reader. In the *Gita*, Krishna commends all those who share his teachings with others. Yet we see how this sharing of the *Gita* can take myriad forms. Just as different translators bring different backgrounds and agendas to their task of rendering Krishna's message, so readers will themselves bring their own differing aims to the work. Among the great plurality of translations, embodying diverse approaches to the *Gita*, the reader also is called on to select a path. If Krishna is correct, all those various translational paths will indeed lead the reader to him and his words.

The *Gita* in Our Time: Performances

CHAPTER 6

Vishnu said: "Wherever the *Bhagavad Gita* is discussed, recited, read, or heard, there I most certainly always dwell. I reside in the *Gita* as my ashram. The *Gita* is my highest home."

— *Gita Mahatmya, verses 6–7*

Religious works do not live simply as words on the page or sentences taken in silently by readers with their eyes. They live also in words uttered with mouths and heard with ears. This is especially so for Indian religious works like the *Bhagavad Gita*. The *Gita* was (according to the *Mahabharata*) an oral dialogue between Krishna and Arjuna, repeated in conversation by Sanjaya to Dhritarashtra, taught orally by Vyasa to his pupils, performed aloud at a court ceremony by Vaishampayana, and retold orally again by Ugrashravas. The *Mahabharata* was (according to most historians) composed as an oral epic and transmitted orally for generations before being put into final written form. So it is fitting to close this account of the life of the *Bhagavad Gita* as it began. In this concluding chapter, we will briefly consider the *Gita* as it is recited and explicated orally in several contemporary settings.[1]

Although the *Bhagavad Gita* has become vastly more available in print over the past century, this proliferation has by no means put an end to oral performances of the text. If anything, the printed work's availability has encouraged and facilitated them. The breadth and variety of *Gita* performances, in India and beyond, is remarkable. They range from simple private household readings, to family and neighborhood recitation sessions, to holy men reciting in temples or at pilgrimage places for passersby, to public *Gita* discourses held almost nightly at halls and auditoriums in every Indian city. Traveling Hindu teachers use the *Gita* for lectures to nonresident Indians around the world, and Hindu temples in the United States conduct classes on the *Gita* for youths to reinforce connections with a "home" culture against the encroaching forces of assimilation. *Gita* performances also take place in numerous college classrooms, like mine, where the *Bhagavad Gita* is presented as a key work for introducing the religion of Hinduism.

The *Gita* may be read aloud as prose, mumbled like a Veda at a fast clip, or chanted in a pleasing repetitive cadence. Trained Indian classical and playback singers, like K. J. Yesudas, may render it as beautiful *sangeet* or song. Ambitious composers may place its words in more dramatic musical settings, such as Douglas Cuomo's 2008 composition *Arjuna's Dilemma*. The 2005 opera by John Adams titled *Doctor Atomic* has the character of Oppenheimer singing translated passages from the *Gita*. And at its most spectacular, Philip Glass's 1980 composition *Satyagraha* employs select verses of the Sanskrit *Gita* sung by Western operatic voices set to the composer's repetitive musical structures, creating a mantra-like evocation of Gandhi's experiences and work in South Africa in the early twentieth century. Thanks to Adams and Glass, opera stages in Rotterdam, Stuttgart, San Francisco, and New York have become temporary ashrams of the *Bhagavad Gita.*

The *Gita's* various audible incarnations are widely available on CDs in Indian music shops, allowing purchasers to become individual audiences to Krishna's words whenever they wish. Nowadays, of course, audio versions are also promiscuous on the Internet. One can quickly find recitations by Swami Prabhupada, Swami Venkatesananda, Prof. Thiagarajan and Sanskrit Scholars (my favorite), and many others. In the United States, the Chinmaya Mission encourages new reciters with an on-line instructional guide to *Gita* chanting, and its centers in Chicago, Boston, New Jersey, and elsewhere hold annual competitions. Chanters are evaluated based on the criteria of memory, pronunciation, and presentation.

As for *Gita* fragments, there is no end. Pieces of the *Gita* and Krishna float through international musical culture. The 1960s were probably the golden age for this. On his posthumous album titled *Om* (released in 1968), John Coltrane and fellow musicians open and close their improvised free jazz composition by chanting a translated passage from the *Gita*. Naturally, there was a 1960s' psychedelic rock group that named itself Bhagavad Gita.

(This obscure group is best known for its recording of "Long Hair Soul.") Jimi Hendrix's famous album cover for *Axis: Bold as Love* (1968) adapted a popular Indian print by B. G. Sharma of Krishna appearing to Arjuna in his Vishvarupa form. And finally, at the dawn of the next decade, the post-Beatles John Lennon declared in his 1970 song "God" that among many other rejected faiths of the 1960s, he didn't believe in "Gita."

It is not possible in this brief work to survey the full range of *Gita* performances. In this chapter, I have presented a few vignettes to illustrate persisting types of contemporary public performance involving the *Bhagavad Gita*.

Prayers at Gandhi's Ashram

Gandhi relocated to Wardha in central India in 1935 at the behest of Jamnalal Bajaj, a Marwari entrepreneur and fervent supporter. In 1936 he moved to Segaon, a small village four miles out of town. For the remaining twelve years of his life Gandhi used this as his primary residence, although he spent much of that time either traveling or in jail. The ashram that grew up around Gandhi there, Sevagram Ashram, still exists as a memorial to Gandhi and his social vision, part ashram and part living museum. The austere bamboo-and-earth structures in which Gandhi and his inner circle lived remain intact: Bapu's hut for Gandhi, Ma's hut for his wife Kasturbai, Mahadev's hut for his secretary

Mahadev Desai, and so on. It is a quiet place with a dozen or so full-time residents now, but it is enlivened by visiting families, schoolchildren on field trips, and the occasional foreign pilgrim.[2]

At the center of the ashram lies the prayer grounds, a simple forty-foot-square area marked off by bamboo poles suspended six inches above the ground. The floor is sand and gravel. A sign identifies it as Gandhi's prayer grounds. Gandhi himself called it a "skyroofed temple" to which followers of all faiths would be welcome. The only request is that footwear be removed as a sign of respect when entering the sacred space.[3] Twice every day, in the early morning and evening, residents and interested visitors assemble for prayer sessions.

At every ashram and wherever he traveled, Gandhi made prayer sessions an integral part of his daily activities.

FIGURE 12. Prayer Grounds at Sevagram Ashram, Wardha. Photograph by the author.

He spoke of prayer as staple food for the soul—an essential means of self-purification. The liturgy of Gandhi's prayer sessions was open ended and ecumenical. It included some Hindu shlokas, hymns, and the repetition of the name Ram (God). It might also include verses from the Quran, and Christian hymns were often sung.

The *Bhagavad Gita* formed a crucial part of the service. Ashram residents would recite a portion of the *Gita* every day, proceeding through the text every fortnight, in order to learn the work by heart. During evening sessions the nineteen verses describing the sthitaprajna, the person of settled wisdom, was an invariable part of the prayers. Gandhi also made use of the prayer assemblies as an occasion to address his ashram coresidents and others. When he presented his most sustained interpretation of the *Gita* in 1926, he did so in oral talks during prayer sessions at Sabarmati Ashram.

Nowadays at Sevagram Ashram, an unoccupied seat back marks the spot where Gandhi used to sit during prayer sessions. Just before 6:00 p.m., participants assemble and sit on mats that have been arranged to face the absent presence of Gandhi. (The nights that I participated, attendance was around forty persons.) A single kerosene lamp is lit as evening gathers. One or two of the regulars spin cotton on portable charkas. The session begins without any clear leader, except the empty seat of Gandhi, and without ceremony. The set of prayers continues Gandhi's policy of religious inclusiveness yet extends it further.[4] First there is a simple Buddhist prayer in Japanese, followed by two minutes of silence. Several Sanskrit prayers are recited next.

Then comes the recitation of the *Bhagavad Gita* section on the sthitaprajna. The participants recite the eleven collective vows of the ashram: nonviolence, truth, nonstealing, and the rest. Next come passages from the holy books of the Muslims, Parsees, Christians, Sikhs, and Jains. Toward the end, a man with a single-stringed instrument leads the group in the call-and-response singing of several devotional songs. We sing Gandhi's favorite, *Ramdhoon*, the recitation of God's names. The liturgy closes with "Om Shanti," a prayer for peace. Without overt ceremony, the participants then get up and leave the prayer grounds.

On the other side of Wardha is Paunar Ashram, first established by Gandhi's prominent acolyte Vinoba Bhave in the 1920s, also with the support of Jamnalal Bajaj. Now the ashram is home to twenty female renouncers and one older male, a member of the Bajaj family. Here too the prayer sessions hark back to Gandhi's ashram practices. The group assembles three times a day on the paved veranda outside the simple empty cell where Vinoba once resided. Since this is where he used to pray, I am told, it is where the nuns prefer to pray. As at Sevagram, the evening prayer always includes the crucial section of the *Gita* devoted to the sthitaprajna. At Paunar, however, it is taken not from the Sanskrit original but rather from Vinoba's Marathi translation, *Gitai* (Mother Gita).[5] Keeping to Gandhi's old strategy for memorization, the women also recite together a chapter of the Sanskrit *Gita* every night. This is done at a fast pace, using well-worn paperback copies of the book. In eighteen nights they can go through the entire work, and then start it all over again.

In Vinoba's ashram things are more identifiably Hindu than at Sevagram. There is not the same conscientious inclusiveness to the liturgy. After prayers, many of the nuns perform a short Hindu worship service in a small shrine nearby. In the shrine, there is an ancient worn stone image, identified as Rama and his brother Bharata from the *Ramayana*, which Vinoba found in the ground during the ashram's construction.

In these Gandhian ashram prayer sessions, the performance of the *Bhagavad Gita* consists of simple daily collective recitation. There is no attempt at musical rendition. There are no living leaders, though the signs of the founders Gandhi and Vinoba are clearly present to all. The text is given no explication, but for those wishing commentary, the written works of Gandhi and Vinoba are readily available at nearby bookstalls. The purpose of such prayer recitation of the *Gita*, as Gandhi set it forth and the ashrams maintain it, is as a regular sustenance for the soul and reiteration of key values shared by the community. By memorizing and reciting the *Gita* daily, ashramites hope to incorporate its values into their lives and become persons whose wisdom is firm.

Discourse at Jnanadeva's Tomb

Alandi is a small pilgrimage city on the Indrayani River, sixteen miles from Pune in Maharashtra. It is here, according to tradition, that the Marathi poet Jnanadeva entered a deep state of meditation and gave up his life. A temple complex now stands on the spot of his *samadhi* (which means both meditation and tomb). There is a stone music hall, the Veena Mandapa, adjacent to the primary shrine. On its walls high above are large painted depictions of Jnanadeva, Tukaram, and other Marathi devotional saints. Subhash Gethe delivers his public *pravachanas* or oral explications on the *Jnaneshvari* here every afternoon at 4:00.

Gethe was born into a family of Jnanadeva devotees, and was educated in both conventional secular institutions and religious ones. While completing BA and MA degrees at the University of Pune, he also finished a four-year training course conducted by a Vaishnava center in Alandi. He wrote his dissertation on the Upanishads and Jnanadeva, and taught philosophy for several years at a college in Pune. Gethe gave up this secular career to live in Alandi, devoting himself full time to becoming an exponent and discourser in the local Vaishnava tradition.[6] When I attended his pravachana session in 2011, I learned that he had spent nearly four years at the temple explicating the nine-thousand-verse *Jnaneshvari* from start to finish, ten to fifteen verses per day, and was within a week of completing the lengthy text.

On the Sunday of my visit, about 150 people fill the music hall and sit cross-legged on the marble floor. The crowd segregates itself, with women sitting to the left of the speaker. This audience appears to be largely a rural or small-town one, and more elderly than young. Many of the men wear white Gandhi caps, typical of this rural area, and the women modestly drape the ends of their saris to cover

FIGURE 13. Subhash Gethe at Alandi, 2011.
Photograph by the author.

their heads. The speaker, dressed in a white kurta and also wearing a Gandhi cap, sits cross-legged on a four-legged platform with a large printed volume of the *Jnaneshvari* placed in a bookstand in front of him. There is a microphone, too, so his lecture can be broadcast throughout the temple courtyard. Except for the microphone, the scene appears much like the setting in which Jnanadeva himself might have delivered his poetic explication of the

Bhagavad Gita, at least as it was reimagined in the popular 1940 Marathi film *Sant Dnyaneshwar*.[7]

Gethe's method of exegesis is straightforward. He reads a single verse from the *Jnaneshvari* and then explains it. Though Jnanadeva composed his poem in a folk song meter, Gethe does not sing the verses, nor is there any instrumental accompaniment. Other devotional modes of performance in Maharashtra, called *kirtana*, feature active congregational singing and musical instruments, but here the emphasis is on the poem as a meaningful text rather than on its musicality. Gethe tells me afterward that he usually spends two hours a day preparing for his one-hour discourse to make sure he understands all the passages. He then speaks without notes. The interaction with the audience is crucial, he says. It is necessary to see the expressions of the listeners and adapt his commentary accordingly. As Jnanadeva puts it, "When my power of speech is fed by attention, a wealth of exposition will come forth in my words."[8] And the audience does respond attentively to Gethe's talk. A few follow along with their own copies of the text. Others sit close to the speaker's platform, reacting with hand gestures of approval and brief verbal assents. Gethe tells me that some in the audience have been attending pravachanas on the *Jnaneshvari* here for twelve or fifteen years, and still relish hearing it again and again.

I try to sit unobtrusively along a side wall, but of course I am visible. I am the only white person present, or anywhere in Alandi, and I am wearing an orange baseball cap instead of Gandhi white. The discourse is in Marathi, but Gethe spots me quickly and enjoys directing an occasional summary to me in English. "Where there is *Gita* and where there is Krishna," he says for my benefit, "there is success." These generous asides to the foreign guest accent the multilingual situation. As Jnanadeva retold and explicated the Sanskrit *Gita* in a thirteenth-century form of poetic Marathi, now difficult for modern speakers, Gethe retells and explains the old Marathi poem in the modern idiom for his contemporary audience, and even in English for his one auditor from the United States. When Gethe completes his day's discourse, many of the audience members touch their foreheads respectfully to the copy of *Jnaneshvari* on the speaker's platform. I do the same.

In contrast to the repetitive daily collective recitation practiced in the Gandhian ashrams, here the *Bhagavad Gita* has become the starting point for a four-year course of explication. Jnanadeva expanded the *Gita* into a lengthy new Marathi devotional poem, and Gethe extends Jnanadeva's poem through his own oral commentary. Although Gethe's training includes secular academic study and teaching, he has chosen to devote himself to an older tradition of Indic discourse, the public oral explication of difficult religious works, still very much alive for the devotionally minded pilgrims of Alandi.

A Modern Shankara in Delhi

The Kamani Auditorium in central Delhi, not far from Connaught Place, advertises itself on its own Web site as "one of the finest halls in India for the presentation of prestigious performances." The modern 632-seat auditorium, a decidedly nonreligious setting, hosts a full program of theater, dance, and musical concerts. In March 2011, Swami Parthasarathy presented a series of five evening lectures on chapter 11 of the *Bhagavad Gita* there to a full house.

A well-traveled and highly successful modern guru, Parthasarathy adapts the nondualist teachings of Shankara's school of Advaita Vedanta to the exigencies of modern life. After a broad education in literature, science, and law, including postgraduate study in international law at University College London, Parthasarathy renounced a promising corporate career to study and teach Vedanta. Over the past forty-some years he has written numerous books, including a three-volume translation and commentary on the *Gita*, and travels widely to address a great variety of audiences.[9] He has conducted Vedanta seminars for international corporations such as Microsoft, Ford, and Merrill Lynch, and at institutions including the World Bank, the Harvard Business School, and the National Aeronautics and Space Administration (NASA). Parthasarathy has worked with the Indian national cricket team and the world's champion in billiards. In 1988 he founded the Vedanta Academy in Malavali, sixty miles outside Mumbai, to convey Vedanta philosophy to students as an encompassing way of life. His organization also maintains centers in eight countries outside India, and at age eighty-two Parthasarathy continues to tour and lecture throughout the world—a vigorous modern Shankara on a global *digvijaya*.

At Kamani Auditorium the lecture is free, but Parthasarathy's books and CDs of his lectures are on sale in the lobby. The audience is largely an urban middle-class Indian one, with a scattering of non-Indians like myself. As the hall fills, the program begins with music. Four young acolytes from the Vedanta Academy, dressed all in white, perform devotional songs on stage, accompanied by harmonium and tabla. A short video presentation on the Vedanta Academy follows, projected from a computer onto a large screen at the side of the stage. Technological tools, conspicuously absent at the Gandhi ashram, are quite evident in this modern auditorium. But Parthasarathy himself projects a simpler image. The slender, dignified South Indian in white kurta walks on to the stage, briefly acknowledges the audience's ovation, sits at a table, and without ceremony or preamble asks for the first verse to be read.

Parthasarathy's discourse covers twelve verses in an hour and a half. Each Sanskrit verse is displayed on the big screen, in Devanagari script and Roman transliteration, and a quartet of female students seated onstage lead the recitation of the verse two times. Most in the audience read along with them. After the recitation, Parthasarathy follows with his comments in English for this mixed cosmopolitan crowd. Parthasarathy holds to a nondualist position, and so in his explication of Arjuna's vision, he stresses that the description of Krishna's all-encompassing form is not the actual shape of God but instead Arjuna's mental projection. So too we all project the world, and our egos lead us to believe that our projections are real and permanent. Arjuna's fearful reaction to his projection dramatizes this common

FIGURE 14. Swami Parthasarathy, lecturing in Ravindra Natya Mandir, Mumbai, 2007.
Photograph courtesy A. Parthasarathy.

misapprehension. Knowledge or comprehension of the underlying brahman, by contrast, can lead to peace. Parthasarathy's impromptu lecture on these central ideas is intellectual yet accessible to his educated audience. Sanskrit terms are at a minimum, but he draws readily on well-known figures and episodes of Hindu tradition. Anecdotes from his travels along with deft, humorous analogies keep the discourse flowing. Though the auditorium stage separates speaker from listeners, Parthasarathy clearly knows his audience—a pious, educated, conscientious, and family-oriented modern Hindu group, confident enough in its values to appreciate some irony and gentle kidding.

In Parthasarathy's hands, the individual verses of the *Bhagavad Gita* serve as points of departure for Vedanta-style commentary. Unlike the medieval sannyasi Shankara, however, Parthasarathy (married for over fifty years) does not urge renunciation as the only path to liberation. Nor is devotion to Krishna seen as an incarnate God emphasized, as medieval theistic Vedantins like Ramanuja did. For those in this urban Delhi audience eager for an understanding suited to their modern worldly lives, Parthasarathy preaches the incorporation of discipline and intellectual clarity into one's existing responsibilities and activities. In keeping with the jnana yoga orientation of Advaita Vedanta, he stresses that this is centrally a matter of developing the intellect. The goals are to eliminate stress, improve concentration and productivity, and live socially useful lives in the modern world. Krishna's teachings to Arjuna, that engaged warrior, serve these purposes well. For modern-day Arjunas, we may envision a manager at Microsoft, an engineer at NASA, an Indian cricketer, or the large attentive audience at the Kamani Auditorium in the Indian capital.

Vedanta in Central Park West

The Vedanta Society of New York occupies a handsome three-story brownstone on Seventy-First Street, a half-block west of Central Park. The society was originally established by Swami Vivekananda and a small coterie of US followers in 1894, one year after his success in Chicago. This makes it the longest-lasting Hindu organization in the United States. In 1921, the society moved to its present comfortable home, donated by Mary Morton, daughter of a former vice president of the United States. Every Friday evening the senior monk Swami Tathagatananda delivers a discourse on the *Bhagavad Gita* in the main chapel here.

Like all Vedanta Society swamis in the United States, Tathagatananda is an unmarried male monk who received his primary training in India, at the Ramakrishna Math in Belur. Tathagatananda came to the United States in 1977 and has lived at the Vedanta Society house for thirty-five years. He has written on numerous subjects, including the book *Journey of the Upanishads to the West* (1994) and several essays on the *Bhagavad Gita*. Now aged eighty-nine and hard of hearing, he continues to present three weekly public lectures: Tuesdays on Ramakrishna, Fridays on the *Gita*, and Sundays on various subjects.

In the chapel, which takes up most of the first floor, a hundred chairs face the front altar, filled with vases of fresh flowers. On the wall above the altar is a handsome print of Ramakrishna, flanked on two side walls by portraits of Vivekananda and Sarada Devi, the founding figures of this spiritual lineage. There are no other icons, though; there are no images or signs of Krishna or any other Hindu deity here. The lights are kept dim, and the atmosphere is quiet and meditative as the small audience assembles. Wearing a salmon-colored monastic robe,

Tathagatananda enters at 8:00 p.m., bows briefly before the image of Ramakrishna, sits quietly for a few minutes in his chair on the dais, adjusts the microphone, and begins his discourse.

He speaks for forty minutes without notes. Tathagatananda's theme is a simple one: we should take time to think about God. The key passage from the *Gita* is Krishna's command to Arjuna (and all of us) near the end of the dialogue. "Keep me in your mind, be my devotee, worship me, honor me, and you will certainly attain me. I promise you this truly, for you are dear to me" (18.65). The swami recites this in Sanskrit and paraphrases it several times. How should we do so? We do not need to envision Krishna as a cowherd boy, Arjuna's companion on the battlefield, or an all-encompassing Absolute. In Tathagatananda's theology, God is found in all life. The fact that we are alive signals the God within us. As an animating spirit God is the very foundation of our being. What prevents us from thinking about God? Basically, we are too caught up in the material world.

Tathagatananda's *Gita* talk is not a sequential commentary on a set portion of the *Bhagavad Gita*, as Parthasarathy's lecture in Delhi, but rather a looser Protestant-style sermon that touches occasionally on the lectionary passage. A few *Gita* verses provide the primary theme, yet along the way the swami weaves in quotations from other gurus: Ramakrishna and Vivekananda, as one would expect, but also Jesus, Gandhi, Abraham Lincoln (a particular favorite of Tathagatananda), Al Gore,

Jimmy Carter, and Arnold Toynbee. Tathagatananda recognizes the *Gita* as a Hindu text, transmitted to the West by the organization founded by Vivekananda, and at the same time he views it as part of a worldwide wisdom tradition. The central aim is to direct our attention away from our enmeshment in mundane affairs toward a contemplation of the living God. Tathagatananda believes that the United States will lead in a new spiritual movement, since Americans have already experienced great affluence and great suffering as well. Gesturing to the New York streets outside the center, he asks me, "What better place to begin than this?"[10]

Kurukshetra: The Next Generation

Meanwhile, back in Kurukshetra, where it was first supposedly uttered, the Shri Krishna Museum celebrates the birthday of the *Bhagavad Gita* with student performances. While the rest of the town hums with an enormous craft fair, cultural performances, and public processions, the museum focuses on educational programs centered around the *Gita*: shloka recitations, quizzes, and "declamations" (*bhasana*). By such means, the *Gita* is transmitted to the next generation.

The Shri Krishna Museum was inaugurated in 1991, as part of an effort by the Kurukshetra Development Board to revive ancient Kurukshetra as a religious and cultural center. Naturally Krishna plays a big role in this promotion. The museum features a wide range of paintings and images of Krishna, depicting all phases of his life, drawn from all regions of India. This is the only museum in the world devoted solely to Krishna, and to my knowledge the only secular museum in India centered on a single Hindu deity. The Kurukshetra Board is also responsible for the massive bronze statue of Krishna and Arjuna nearby and for the Kurukshetra Festival coinciding with Gita Jayanti. Over the past two decades the festival has grown enormously.

Since the 1990s, the museum has organized *Gita* programs during the festival involving several types of competitive performances. First there were shloka recitations by younger students. Next the museum added a quiz contest for high school students, in which the contestants would match their knowledge of the *Gita*, the *Mahabharata*, and general Indian cultural information. Third came a *Gita* bhasana competition for students at the college level. The competitors would compose and deliver brief declamations on assigned topics pertaining to the *Gita*. The museum's curator, R. S. Rana, hopes to introduce a fourth kind of competitive program in the future, which he calls *Gita-samvada-pratiyogita*, or a staged *Gita* dialogue. High school students costumed as Krishna and Arjuna would recite appropriate shlokas from the *Gita*, and be judged on all aspects of their presentation and performance.[11]

My visit coincides with the *Gita* declamation contest. The museum auditorium is filled with about 150 students from nearby secondary schools, dressed in their blue-checked and red-sweater school uniforms.

On the dais in front sit three judges, all local educators, and the chief guest, a distinguished retired university professor of philosophy. As a visiting foreign guest, I am also asked to sit in front. This is an Indian public event, and certain protocols are required before the actual competition can begin. There are lengthy laudatory introductions, and the chief guest presents a speech. I am asked to say a few auspicious words. Then the contest can start.

The finalists in the competition have been given five possible topics: the *Gita* and righteous conduct, *Gita* as the essence of the Upanishads, the catholicity of the *Gita*, the role of the *Gita* in management, or the role of the *Gita* in the freedom movement. The contestants are asked to give an address of five to seven minutes on one of these. As it turns out, all the speakers address either management or the freedom movement.

The winning declamation concerns the application of the *Gita* to management. The speaker takes as his key passage Krishna's explanation for his avatara: "For whenever there is a decline in righteousness and an increase in unrighteousness, Arjuna, then I emanate myself. For the protection of good people, for the destruction of evil-doers, and for the restoration of righteousness, I take birth in age after age" (4.7–8). Just as Krishna incarnates himself when dharma is threatened, the effective manager must intervene whenever there is instability within the organization. Krishna is manager and motivator to Arjuna, and the young speaker effectively points to many places where Krishna's battlefield teachings may apply to modern management. As Krishna emphasizes the need for mental single-mindedness, the manager is responsible for instilling and sustaining organizational focus. Krishna's principle of nonattachment to the fruits of action is also relevant to the manager, who must keep the organization's broad objective in mind without undue attachment to immediately monetary outcomes. Krishna counsels the manager to maintain the long view.

The winning contestant reflects one of the latest developments in the life of the *Bhagavad Gita*. Both in India and abroad, the *Gita* has entered a new Kurukshetra: the corporate world. New management gurus (another Indic term now in the common English lexicon) have adapted Krishna's instructions to the warrior Arjuna to the requirements of business executives and managers. The success of Swami Parthasarathy as a corporate consultant is one clear example. In American business schools, professors like Vijay Govindarajan at Dartmouth and the late C. K. Prahalad at the University of Michigan have deployed the *Gita* in their class and consultation performances, much as other business gurus have redirected the war teachings of Carl von Clausewitz and Sun Tzu.

In India, the best-known exemplar of *Gita*-infused management is Elattuvalapil Sreedharan, who served until recently as managing director of the Delhi Metro. Sreedharan follows a personal discipline, he tells me, of spending a half hour every day reading and contemplating verses from the *Gita*, three to five verses each day. In twelve or so years, he has been through the text twelve times in his morning study. To help create a strong institutional ethos of duty and public service, Sreedharan distributed copies of the *Gita Makaranda*, a translation of the *Gita* with a lengthy commentary by Swami Vidyaprakashananda, to all management-level personnel in the organization. In this new institutional setting, the *Gita* is not a "Hindu text," insists Sreedharan, but rather an "administrative gospel," a conversation between two administrators on a battlefield that covers all important topics for organizational well-being.[12]

Visual Performance: *Shri Krishna Arjun Rath*

In India, the *Bhagavad Gita* lives also in visual form. Though relatively uncommon in medieval sculpture, Krishna of the *Gita* has been reincarnated visually during the twentieth and twenty-first centuries in nearly endless array. Krishna and Arjuna ride their chariot along the walls of upscale restaurants and hotels throughout India. In the popular mass-produced genre of religious prints known as "calendar prints" or "God pictures," treatments of Krishna as he appears in the *Bhagavad Gita* have been prominent since the 1920s and 1930s, paralleling the growing interest in the work promoted by Indian leaders like Tilak and Gandhi. In God pictures, two *Gita* themes predominate, reflecting the two sides of Krishna's identity—human charioteer and Supreme Deity. In the first type, Krishna and Arjuna in the chariot either converse or ride into battle, often with a shloka or two from the Sanskrit text alongside. In the second, Krishna rises before Arjuna in his supernal Vishvarupa form, filling the frame with his countless arms and heads.

The largest new three-dimensional incarnation, however, appears appropriately at Kurukshetra, site of the ancient battle. This is a sixty-foot-long, thirty-five-foot-high, forty-five-ton bronze sculpture, *Shri Krishna Arjun Rath*, created in 2007 by Ram V. Sutar and his son Anil R. Sutar.[13] Arjuna stands in an elaborate two-wheeled chariot drawn by four horses. A strapping warrior figure in armor and cape, holding a bow in one hand and a sword in the other, Arjuna looks forward toward his charioteer. A human Krishna sits holding the reins, as if listening intently to his interlocutor. The scene depicts the dramatic moment at the onset of the *Gita*, when Arjuna first expresses his anxieties to Krishna, in the heroic form through which Indian public art envisions its national past.

The sculpture germinated in the Ministry of Tourism of the Indian central government. To assist Kurukshetra in its efforts to become a more inviting destination for pilgrims and tourists, the ministry decided to sponsor a large *Gita*-based public artwork. It invited bids, and selected the firm of Ram Sutar Fine Arts for the commission. An esteemed Delhi-based artist, Ram Sutar specializes in large-scale sculpture, and has created numerous statues of Gandhi and other public leaders as well as works on religious themes. Due to its large size, the *Shri*

FIGURE 15. *Shri Krishna Arjun Rath*, bronze sculpture by Ram V. Sutar and Anil R. Sutar, Kurukshetra, Haryana, 2007. Photograph by the author.

Krishna Arjun Rath was cast in parts in the firm's foundry in Noida (Delhi), then transported and assembled on-site in Kurukshetra. Originally the work was intended for Jyotisar, but evidently the cost of moving it once assembled was prohibitive, and so it stands overlooking the Brahmasarovar, the large pilgrimage lake in the center of town. Sonia Gandhi, president of the Congress Party, inaugurated the statue in July 2008. The *Shri Krishna Arjun Rath* has quickly become one of the signature sights of Kurukshetra.

In the modern Indian economy, the *Bhagavad Gita* has been recruited to promote tourism. Building on the growth of the annual *Gita* birthday festival and the showcase sculpture, the Haryana State Tourist Board has decided now to sponsor another massive piece of artwork for Kurukshetra. This one will be a bronze sculpture, forty feet in height, of Krishna as he appears to Arjuna in his all-encompassing form, "Virat Roop." The Ram Sutar firm has submitted its bid, along with other competing sculptural companies. As of this writing, the winning design has not been selected.

The *Bhagavad Gita* in Great Time

"Works break through the boundaries of their own time," writes Russian literary theorist Mikhail Bakhtin. "They live in centuries, that is, in *great time*, and frequently (with great works always) their lives are more intense and fuller than are their lives within their own time."[1] In this survey, we have observed the intense and full life that the *Bhagavad Gita* has lived, starting from its own time. The life of this work took shape as part of a larger composition, the great Sanskrit poem *Mahabharata*. The discussion of two important figures of the epic at the onset of a cataclysmal war touched on central themes and tensions within the story. Krishna's teachings drew on ideas and disputes of classical India, restating and reformulating them into an innovative synthesis. The complexity of Krishna's message and his reconciliation of multiple religious pathways (as Vivekananda and others have phrased it) spoke powerfully to audiences of the *Gita*'s own time of composition. It also made for a work rich in significance and susceptible to multiple interpretations.

Although a great work of religious literature speaks within and to its own time of composition, Bakhtin reminds us that such a work cannot be closed off in this epoch. Its fullness, he observes, is revealed only in "great time." In this continuing life, the work comes to be enriched with new meanings and new relevance by new readers in new settings. Different aspects may come to the fore, and these too become part of the life of the text. In medieval India, new hearers and readers found ways that the work spoke to their concerns. For Vedanta commentators like Shankara and Ramanuja, the *Gita* addressed central theological debates. In the hands of the Maharashtrian bhakti poet Jnanadeva, Krishna's Sanskrit dialogue with Arjuna proliferated into a greatly expanded devotional *Gita* in vernacular Marathi. In late nineteenth- and early twentieth-century colonial India, nationalist writers and political figures revisited the *Gita*. They promoted it as a central work of an emerging Indian national ethos, and discovered in it strong advocacy for engaged social and political action, although the form that action should take remained a point of heated contention.

Just as religious works may break through the boundaries of their own time of composition, some also reach beyond their original culture. The *Bhagavad Gita* may have originated in the Hinduism of classical India, but it has assuredly not been confined to it. The *Gita*'s passage out of India began most notably with Wilkins's translation, which rendered the Sanskrit verse work into eighteenth-century English prose. The English *Bhagavat-Geeta* delivered the work to an altogether-new audience that eventually included British colonial officials, German romantics, and transcendentalists in the United States. European observers took the *Gita* as both an ancient book of timeless wisdom and the primary representative work through which to understand and evaluate Hinduism and Indian religious culture.

Wilkins's translation was only the first of many. Through its myriad translations into English and other languages of the world in the past two centuries, the *Gita* has become a global scripture. Some scholarly translations attempt to recover the *Gita* as a historical composition, but many more seek to present the work as a still-living poem. What that poem wishes most to say, however, remains a matter of diverse interpretation. In modern India and beyond, the *Gita* also continues to lead a rich performative life, including recitations, musical adaptations, oral explications, and dramatized renderings. Audiences continue to read and listen closely to the *Gita* and to its new commentators, seeking guidance as they navigate complex worldly lives.

Where will the *Bhagavad Gita* go in the future? During the several years that I have been researching its past, the *Gita* has continued to appear periodically in the news. Recent events in India, Russia, and the United States reflect some of the current status of the *Gita*, and perhaps give some indication of its future directions.

In 2011, V. H. Kageri, an education minister in the southern Indian state of Karnataka, proposed that teaching the *Bhagavad Gita* be made compulsory in the state school system. The ideal would be to devote one hour per day of class time to the *Gita*, he opined. His suggestion reflected the Hindu nationalist orientation of the party in power in Karnataka, the Bharatiya Janata Party. "I think it is the duty of every Indian to respect the *Bhagavad Gita*," Kageri stated. "I strongly feel that if someone does not respect it they have no place in India. They should leave the country and settle abroad." For Kageri, the *Gita* is a key maker of Indian identity. Other groups in Karnataka quickly objected. The *Gita* is a Hindu religious work, they countered. India is a secular country, and it is inappropriate to require all students to study a sacred text of one religious community. In 2012, the chief minister of Karnataka, D. V. Sadananda Gowda, continued to push for expanded *Gita* teaching in the public schools, but he adopted a softer rhetorical tact. The *Gita*, he argued, "doesn't belong to a particular religion or a sect as its teachings are universal. It aims at refining mankind, and other religions have appreciated its philosophical teachings." In contemporary India, the question of the *Gita*'s fundamental identity—whether it be Hindu, Indian, or universally human—persists as a matter of public debate.

Outside India, too, the *Bhagavad Gita* can provoke controversy. In June 2011, in Tomsk, Russia, state prosecutors brought a case against the *Gita*. Specifically, they sought to ban a Russian translation of *Bhagavad Gita As It Is* by Swami Prabhupada on charges of religious extremism. The prosecution contended that the work is extremist because it makes a claim for the exclusiveness of the Krishna religion, is anti-Christian by nature, and fosters social discord, religious hatred, and discrimination. Evidently the case was instigated by the local branch of the Russian Orthodox Church, which wished to restrict the proselytizing activities of ISKCON, the Hare Krishna devotional organization. In an earlier case, when ISKCON sought permission to construct a Hindu temple in Moscow, the church opposed it vehemently, labeling Krishna an "evil demon." The stakes were high. If a book is guilty of religious extremism, then possession of that work becomes a punishable offense.

The case evoked a storm of criticism, and drew Russian and Indian diplomats into the fray. In India, members of parliament vented their anger over the case in the Lok Sabha. "We will not tolerate any move to insult Lord Krishna," exclaimed one Indian politician. They demanded that the Indian government intervene. The Russian ambassador in India expressed his public regret. He reiterated that Russia is a secular and democratic nation, and stressed that the *Gita* itself was not on trial, only Prabhupada's "imperfect" commentaries on it. The Indian ambassador in Russia observed that the *Gita* was "perhaps the most important and respected scripture in the world." Russian authorities, he stated, had been urged by Indian officials "at a high level" to resolve the matter appropriately. So in many quarters sighs of relief came on December 28, 2011, when the Russian court in Tomsk rejected the prosecutors' case. In Russia, neither the *Bhagavad Gita* nor Prabhupada's commentary on it is legally considered a work of religious extremism.

In Washington, DC, Tulsi Gabbard was sworn in on January 2013 as the first Hindu member of the United States Congress. Her father is Catholic and her mother is Hindu, and Gabbard says she embraced the Hindu side of her heritage as a teenager. To take the oath of office, Representative Gabbard chose to place her hand on a personal copy of the *Bhagavad Gita*.

Although no religious ceremony is required, Christian and Jewish members of Congress frequently utilize the bibles of their respective traditions when being sworn in. In 2007 Keith Ellison, the first Muslim member of Congress, had used a copy of the Quran (and one originally belonging to Thomas Jefferson) for his oath. Gabbard did not characterize the *Gita* as the "Hindu Bible" but instead described it as a work of personal inspiration. She chose it, she said, because its teachings had inspired her "to strive to be a servant-leader, dedicating my life in the service of others and to my country." During her service in Iraq, she went on, surrounded by visible reminders of mortality, she derived special strength and reassurance from Krishna's battlefield teachings to Arjuna on the indestructibility of the soul. Among her favorite *Gita* verses, she quoted this one: "The soul can never be cut into pieces by any weapon, nor can it be burned by fire, nor moistened by water, nor withered by wind" (2.23). Although her Republican opponent had asserted during the campaign that her Hindu faith was incompatible with the US Constitution, no public objection was made to Gabbard's introduction of the *Bhagavad Gita* into the halls of the US capitol.

This exploration of the *Bhagavad Gita*'s biography is part of that life, too. In reviewing some of the ways that the *Gita* has lived over the centuries, we have seen how the work has spoken in multiple new ways to new audiences. As Bakhtin writes, "There is neither a first word nor a last work. . . . Even meanings born in dialogues of the remotest past will never be grasped once and for all, for they will always be renewed in later dialogue."[2] We may be certain that this text will continue to reincarnate itself in new ways. Or as Vishnu puts it in the *Gita Mahatmya*, these will all be part of his "highest home" in great time.

CHAPTER I

The *Bhagavad Gita* in the Time of Its Composition

1. Among several accessible retellings of the *Mahābhārata*, the most reliable is C. V. Narasimhan, *The Mahābhārata* (New York: Columbia University Press, 1973). Somewhere between retelling and translation is the highly abridged but useful eight-hundred-page *Mahābhārata* by John D. Smith, *The Mahābhārata: An Abridged Translation* (London: Penguin Books, 2009). For a partial full translation, see the ongoing University of Chicago Press project, translations by J.A.B. Van Buitenen and James Fitzgerald, *The Mahābhārata*, 4 vols. (Chicago: University of Chicago Press, 1973–2004). Finally, a full translation was completed in the 1890s by Kisari Mohan Ganguly, and is available in a reprint edition: Kisan Mohan Ganguly, *Mahabharata of Krishna-Dwaipayana Vyasa*, 4 vols. (Delhi: Munshiram Manoharlal, 2004).

2. All quotations from the *Bhagavad Gītā* cited parenthetically in the text will hereafter refer to chapter and verse numbers only.

3. On Vyasa, see Bruce M. Sullivan, *Seer of the Fifth Veda: Kṛṣṇa Dvaipāyana Vyāsa in the Mahābhārata* (Delhi: Motilal Banarsidass, 1999); Alf Hiltebeitel, *Rethinking the Mahābhārata: A Reader's Guide to the Education of the Dharma King* (Chicago: University of Chicago Press, 2001).

4. For notable recent scholarship concerning the composition and date of the *Mahābhārata*, see J.A.B. Van Buitenen, *The Mahābhārata*, vol. 1 (Chicago: University of Chicago Press, 1973); Madeleine Biardeau, *Le Mahābhārata: un récit fondateur du brahmanisme et son interprétation*, 2 vols. (Paris: Seuil, 2002); Hiltebeitel, *Rethinking the Mahābhārata*; James L. Fitzgerald, *The Mahābhārata*, vol. 7 (Chicago: University of Chicago Press, 2004); Angelika Malinar, *The Bhagavadgītā: Doctrines and Contexts* (Cambridge: Cambridge University Press, 2007).

5. On the monumental project of critically editing the *Mahābhārata*, see the collected essays of the first project director, Vishnu Shankar Sukthankar, *Critical Studies in the Mahābhārata* (Poona: V. S. Sukthankar Memorial Committee, 1944). For a brief postcolonial take on the project, see Peter van der Veer, *Imperial Encounters: Religion and Modernity in India and Britain* (Princeton, NJ: Princeton University Press, 2001), 116–22.

6. J.A.B. Van Buitenen, *The Bhagavad Gītā in the Mahābhārata* (Chicago: University of Chicago Press, 1981), 5–6. See also Franklin Edgerton, *The Bhagavad Gītā* (Cambridge, MA: Harvard University Press, 1944).

CHAPTER 2
Krishna and His *Gita* in Medieval India

1. I am grateful to Jack Hawley for extensive comments on an earlier draft of this chapter.

2. *Mahābhārata*, *Sabhāparvan*, chaps. 34–42. See J.A.B. Van Buitenen, *Mahābhārata* (Chicago: University of Chicago Press, 1975), 2:93–106.

3. For accessible translations of the Krishna portions of the *Harivaṃśa* and *Bhāgavata Purāṇa*, see Francis G. Hutchins, *Young Krishna* (West Franklin, NH: Amarta Press, 1980); Edwin F. Bryant, *Krishna: The Beautiful Legend of God* (London: Penguin Books, 2003).

4. Friedhelm Hardy, *Viraha-Bhakti. The Early History of Kṛṣṇa Devotion in South India* (Delhi: Oxford University Press, 1983).

5. John S. Hawley, "Krishna's Cosmic Victories," *Journal of the American Academy of Religion* 47 (1979): 201–21.

6. For general treatments of this genre, see Umesh Chandra Bhattacharjee, "The Gītā Literature and Its Relation with Brahma-Vidyā," *Indian Historical Quarterly* 2 (1926): 537–46, 761–71; R. Nilakantan, *Gītās in the Mahābhārata and the Purāṇas* (Delhi: Nag Publishers, 1989). For translated examples of other gods' gītās, see Greg Bailey, *Gaṇeśapurāṇa* (Wiesbaden: Otto Harrassowitz Verlag, 1995); C. Mackenzie Brown, *The Devī Gītā: The Song of the Goddess* (Albany, NY: SUNY Press, 1998); Steven J. Rosen, *Krishna's Other Song: A New Look at the Uddhava Gita* (Santa Barbara, CA: Praeger, 2010); Andrew J. Nicholson, *Lord Śiva's Song: The Īśvara Gītā* (Albany, NY: SUNY Press, 2014).

7. *Bhagavadgītā with Śāṅkarabhāṣya* (Delhi: Motilal Banasidass, 1988), 1–2. For a full English translation, see A. Mahadeva Sastri, *The Bhagavad-Gītā with the Commentary of Śrī Śaṇkarāchārya* (Mysore: G.T.A. Printing Works, 1901).

8. Winand Callewaert and Shilanand Hemraj, *Bhagavadgītānuvāda: A Study in Transcultural Translation* (Ranchi: Satya Bharati Publications, 1982), 98–110. For sixty-four Sanskrit commentaries, see also the index in Karl H. Potter, *Encyclopedia of Indian Philosophies: Bibliography* (Princeton, NJ: Princeton University Press, 1983), 946–47.

9. For a general introduction to the Vedanta schools, see R. N. Dandekar, "Vedanta," in *The Encyclopedia of Religion*, ed. Mircea Eliade (New York: Macmillan, 1987), 16:207–14. For a valuable summary of several Vedanta commentaries on the *Gītā*, see Arvind Sharma,

The Hindu Gītā: Ancient and Classical Interpretations of the Bhagavadgītā (LaSalle, IL: Open Court Publishing, 1986). For a fuller treatment, see T. G. Mainkar, *A Comparative Study of the Commentaries on the Bhagavadgītā* (Delhi: Motilal Banarsidass, 1969).

10. Gary A. Tubb and Emery R. Boose, *Scholastic Sanskrit: A Handbook for Students* (New York: American Institute of Buddhist Studies at Columbia University, 2007), 1.

11. A. Govindacharya, *Sri Bhagavad-gītā with Sri Rāmānujāchārya's Viṣisthādvaita Commentary* (Madras: Vaijayanti Press, 1898); J.A.B. Van Buitenen, *Rāmānuja on the Bhagavadgītā: A Condensed Rendering of His Gītābhāṣya with Copious Notes and an Introduction* (The Hague: Ned Bock en Steendrukkerji, 1958). For an excellent overview of Rāmānuja's viewpoint, see John Braisted Carman, *The Theology of Rāmānuja: An Essay in Interreligious Understanding* (New Haven, CT: Yale University Press, 1974).

12. Van Buitenen, *Rāmānuja on the Bhagavadgītā*, 45–47.

13. Sheldon I. Pollock, *The Language of the Gods in the World of Men: Sanskrit, Culture, and Power in Premodern India* (Berkeley: University of California Press, 2006).

14. All quotations from Swami Kripananda, *Jnaneshwar's Gita: A Rendering of the Jnaneshwari* (Albany, NY: SUNY Press, 1989); it is based on the translation by V. G. Pradhan, *Jnāneshvari: Bhavārthadipikā, Written by Shri Jnāneshvar* (Albany, NY: SUNY Press, 1987). I am grateful to Christian Novetzke and Jon Keune for valuable comments on a longer draft chapter on Jñānadeva and his work.

CHAPTER 3

Passages from India

1. Walt Whitman, *Leaves of Grass* (New York: Viking Press, 1959). "Passage to India" was first added to the fifth edition (1871) of *Leaves of Grass* as an appendix.

2. George Hendrick, "Whitman's Copy of the Bhagavad-Gita," *Walt Whitman Review* 5 (1959): 12–14.

3. On Wilkins's career, see Mary Lloyd, "Sir Charles Wilkins, 1749–1836), *India Office Library and Records Report* (1978): 9–39. For his contributions to Sanskrit studies, see E. H. Johnston, "Charles Wilkins," in *Woolner Commemoration Volume*, ed. M. Shafi (Lahore: Meherchand Lachman Das, 1940). See also Richard H. Davis, "Wilkins, Kasinatha, Hastings, and the First English Gita," special issue honoring Edwin Gerow, *International Journal of Hindu Studies* (forthcoming). I am grateful to Brian Hatcher and Rosane Rocher for their valuable comments on a longer essay on Wilkins and Kashinatha.

4. Charles Wilkins, *A Grammar of the Sanskrita Language* (London: C. Nourse, 1808), xi. On Halhed's oriental career, see Rosane Rocher, *Orientalism, Poetry, and the Millennium: The Checkered Life of Nathaniel Brassey Halhed, 1751–1830* (Delhi: Motilal Banaridass, 1983).

5. Charles Wilkins, "A Catalogue of Sanscita Manuscripts Presented to the Royal Society by Sir William and Lady Jones (1798)," in vol. 13, *The Works of Sir William Jones* (Delhi: Agam Prakashan, 1980).

6. Charles Wilkins, *The Bhagavat-Gēētā, or Dialogues of Kreeshna and Arjoon, in Eighteen Lectures; with Notes* (London: C. Nourse, 1785), 24–25.

7. Ibid., 24.

8. P. J. Marshall, *The British Discovery of Hinduism in the Eighteenth Century* (Cambridge: Cambridge University, 1970), 12.

9. Sydney G. Grier, *The Letters of Warren Hastings to His Wife* (Edinburgh: William Blackwood and Sons, 1905), 364–65.

10. Warren Hastings, "To Nathaniel Smith, Esquire," in *The Bhagavat-Gēētā, or Dialogues of Kreeshna and Arjoon*, ed. Charles Wilkins (London: C. Nourse, 1785), 10.

11. For the broadest account of the European response to works of Indian antiquity during this period, see Raymond Schwab, *The Oriental Renaissance: Europe's Rediscovery of India and the East, 1680–1880* (New York: Columbia University Press). On the response in German, see A. Leslie Willson, *A Mythical Image: The Ideal of India in German Romanticism* (Durham, NC: Duke University Press, 1964); Wilhelm Halbfass, *India and Europe: An Essay in Understanding* (Albany, NY: SUNY Press, 1988); Bradley L. Herling, *The German Gita: Hermeneutics and Discipline in the German Reception of Indian Thought, 1778–1831* (New York: Routledge, 2006); Vishwa Adluri and Jagdeep Bagchee, *The Nay Science: A History of German Indology* (New York: Oxford University Press, 2014). For a work tracing the *Gītā* in the poetry of the English Romantics, see K. G. Srivastava, *Bhagavad-Gītā and the English Romantic Movement* (Delhi: Macmillan India Ltd., 2002).

12. Quoted in Schwab, *Oriental Renaissance*, 71.

13. Quoted in ibid., 161.

14. Rosane Rocher, *Alexander Hamilton (1762–1824): A Chapter in the Early History of Sanskrit Philology* (New Haven, CT: American Oriental Society, 1968).

15. Friedrich von Schlegel, *The Aesthetic and Miscellaneous Works of Friedrich von Schlegel*, trans. E. J. Millington (London: Henry G. Bohn, 1849), 427.

16. Henry David Thoreau, *Walden, or, Life in the Woods* (New York: Alfred A. Knopf, 1992). On Thoreau and the *Gita*, see Robert D. Richardson Jr., *Henry Thoreau: A Life of the Mind* (Berkeley: University of California Press, 1986); Paul Friedrich, *The Gita within Walden* (Albany, NY: SUNY Press, 2006); Barbara Stoller Miller, "Afterword: Why Did Henry David Thoreau Take the *Bhagavad-Gita* to Walden Pond," in *The Bhagavad-gita: Krishna's Counsel in Time of War*, trans.

Barbara Stoller Miller (New York. Columbia University Press, 1986).

17. For an example of missionary *Gītā* reading, see J. N. Farquhar, *Gītā and Gospel* (Madras: Christian Literature Society, 1917); it portrays the *Gītā* as "the cry of the Hindu people for an incarnate Saviour" (32). For more recent Christian reflections on the *Gītā*, see Catherine Cornille, ed., *Song Divine: Christian Commentaries on the Bhagavad Gītā* (Leuven: Peeters, 2006).

18. Quoted in Wilkins, *Bhagavat Gēētā*, 13. On Hastings's role in promoting early Indological knowledge, see P. J. Marshall, "Warren Hastings as Scholar and Patron," in *Statesmen, Scholars, and Merchants: Essays in Eighteenth Century History Presented to Dame Lucy Sutherland*, ed. Anne Bramley J. S. Whiteman and P.G.M. Dickenson (Oxford: Clarendon Press, 1973), 342–62.

19. James Mill, *The History of British India* (London: Baldwin, Cradock and Joy, 1826). On Mill and Grant as examples of "Indophobia," see Thomas R. Trautmann, *Aryans and British India* (Berkeley: University of California Press, 1997).

20. Terence Ball, "James Mill," in *Oxford Dictionary of National Biography*, ed. H.C.G. Matthew and Brian Harrison (Oxford: Oxford University Press, 2004), 38:150.

21. Mill, *History of British India*, 329–30.

22. Ibid., 283.

23. Herling, *The German Gita*, 168.

24. Herbert Herring, introduction to *On the Episode of the Mahābhārata Known by the Name Bhagavad-Gītā by Wilhelm von Humboldt*, by Georg Wilhelm Friedrich Hegel (New Delhi: Indian Council of Philosophical Research, 1995), xiv–xv.

25. Georg Wilhelm Friedrich Hegel, *On the Episode of the Mahābhārata Known by the Name Bhagavad-Gītā by Wilhelm von Humboldt*, trans. Herbert Herring (New Delhi: Indian Council of Philosophical Research, 1995).

26. Richard Hughes Seager, *The World's Parliament of Religions: The East/West Encounter, Chicago, 1893* (Bloomington: Indiana University Press, 1995).

27. Marie Louise Burke, *Swami Vivekananda in America: New Discoveries* (Calcutta: Advaita Ashrama, 1958). For general biographies of Vivekananda, see Eastern and Western Disciples, *The Life of Swami Vivekananda*, 3rd ed. (1912; repr., Mayavati, Himalayas: Advaita Ashrama, 1944); Christopher Isherwood, *Ramakrishna and His Disciples* (London: Metheuen and Co., 1965). I am grateful to Gordon Stavig (Gopal) for his comments on this section.

28. Disciples, *Life of Swami Vivekananda*, 363.

29. This is Vivekananda's rendering of *Bhagavad Gītā* 4.11. For his addresses at the parliament, see Swami Vivekananda, *The Complete Works of Swami Vivekananda*, 8 vols. (Calcutta: Advaita Ashrama, 1970–73), 1:3–24. On Vivekananda and the *Gītā*, see Harold W. French, "Swami Vivekananda's Use of the *Bhagavadgita*," in *Modern Indian Interpreters of the Bhagavadgita*, ed. R. N. Minor (Albany, NY: SUNY Press, 1986), 131–46.

30. Swami Nikhilananda, *Vivekananda: A Biography* (New York: Ramakrishna-Vivekananda Center, 1953), 60.

31. Carl T. Jackson, *Vedanta for the West: The Ramakrishna Movement in the United States* (Bloomington: Indiana University Press, 1994).

32. Vivekananda, "Madras Lecture," in *Complete Works*, 3:242.

33. Nikhilananda, *Vivekananda: A Biography*, 69.

CHAPTER 4
Krishna, the *Gita*, and the Indian Nation

1. Swami Shraddhananda, *Hindu Sangathan: Saviour of the Dying Race* (Delhi: Arjun Press, 1926), 130–41. On Shraddhananda's career, see J.T.F. Jordens, *Swami Shraddhananda: His Life and Causes* (Delhi: Oxford University Press, 1981). I thank Jyotindra Jain for bringing this

work to my attention. I also thank Philip Oldenberg and Sanjib Baruah for useful comments on an earlier draft of this chapter.

2. The most prominent examples are the Gita Mandirs in both Kurukshetra and Mathura and the Gita Bhavan in Delhi, constructed in the 1930s and 1940s by the industrialist Birla family, strong supporters of Gandhi and also Hindu nationalist leaders like Madan Mohan Malaviya.

3. Bankimchandra Chattopadhyay, *Krishna-Charitra*, trans. Pradip Bhattacharya (Calcutta: M. P. Birla Foundation, 1991), 21.

4. James Mill, *The History of British India* (London: Baldwin, Cradock, and Joy, 1826), 1:144.

5. Monier Monier-Williams, *Brahmanism and Hinduism; or, Religious Thought and Life in India*, 4th ed. (New York: Macmillan and Co., 1891), 136.

6. Lala Lajpat Rai, "Great Men of the World: V. Shri Krishna," in *The Collected Works of Lala Lajpat Rai*, ed. B. R. Nanda (Delhi: Manohar Publishers, 2003), 1:434.

7. Ibid., 1:430.

8. Ibid., 1:434.

9. Ibid., 1:435.

10. Lala Lajpat Rai, "Message of the *Bhagwad Gita*," in *The Collected Works of Lala Lajpat Rai*, ed. B. R. Nanda (Delhi: Manohar Publishers, 2003), 3:329–53. On karma yoga and Indian nationalism, see Ursula King, "Who Is the Ideal Karmayogin? The Meaning of a Hindu Religious Symbol," *Religion* 10 (1980): 41–45; Dilip Bose, "Bhagavad-Gita and Our National Movement," in *Marxism and the Bhagvat Geeta* (New Delhi: People's Publishing House, 1982); V. Subrahmaniam, "Karmayoga and the Rise of the Indian Middle Class," *Journal of Arts and Ideas* 14–15 (1987): 133–42. See also the recent work of K. Nagappa Gowda, *The Bhagavadgita in the Nationalist Discourse* (New Delhi: Oxford University Press, 2011).

11. Lajpat Rai, "Message of the *Bhagwad Gita*," 353.

12. Uma Mukherjee, *Two Great Indian Revolutionaries: Rosh Behari Bose and Jyotindra Nath Mukherjee* (Calcutta: Firma K. L. Mukhopadhyay, 1966), 17. For secondary accounts of the Anushilan Samiti, see R. C. Majumdar, *History of the Freedom Movement in India*, 3 vols. (Calcutta: Firma K. L. Mukhopadhyay, 1963), 2:265–327; Leonard A. Gordon, *Bengal: The Nationalist Movement, 1876–1940* (New York: Columbia University Press, 1974), 135–60.

13. James Campbell Ker, *Political Trouble in India, 1907–1917* (Delhi: Oriental Publishers, 1973), 50. A senior officer working as a personal assistant to the director of criminal intelligence, Ker compiled all available information in this 1917 confidential report on the various Indian revolutionary groups active in the first two decades of the twentieth century.

14. For excellent biographies detailing the career of Aurobindo Ghose, see Peter Heehs, *Sri Aurobindo: A Brief Biography* (Delhi: Oxford University Press, 1989); and Peter Heehs, *The Lives of Sri Aurobindo* (New York: Columbia University Press, 2008). For Aurobindo's early political writings, see Aurobindo Ghose, *Bande Mataram: Early Political Writings—1* (Pondicherry: Sri Aurobindo Ashram Press, 1972); Aurobindo Ghose, *Karmayogin: Early Political Writings—2* (Pondicherry: Sri Aurobindo Ashram Press, 1972).

15. Aurobindo Ghose, "Bombay Speech," quoted in Heehs, *Sri Aurobindo*, 91.

16. For a full historical study of this key Indian nation-deity, see Sumathi Ramaswamy, *The Goddess and the Nation: Mapping Mother India* (Durham, NC: Duke University Press, 2010).

17. Bal Gangadhar Tilak, *Śrīmad Bhagavadgītā-rahasya, or Karma-yoga-śāstra*, trans. B. S. Sukthankar (Poona: Tilak

Brothers, 1935). On Tilak's interpretation of the *Gītā*, see D. Mackenzie Brown, "The Philosophy of Bal Gangadhar Tilak: *Karma* vs. *Jñāna* in the *Gītā Rahasya*," *Journal of Asian Studies* 17 (1957–58): 197–206.

18. For a good overview of Hedgwar's career and primary works, see G. S. Hingle, *Hindutva Reawakened* (New Delhi: Vikas Publishing House, 1999). On the RSS, see Walter K. Andersen and Shridhar D. Damle, *The Brotherhood in Saffron: The Rashtriya Swayamsevak Sangh and Hindu Revivialism* (Boulder, CO: Westview Press, 1987). For a broader history of Hindu nationalism, see Christophe Jaffrelot, *The Hindu Nationalist Movement in India* (New York: Columbia University Press, 1996).

19. Nagappa Gowda, *Bhagavadgita in the Nationalist Discourse*, 222–35.

20. Mohandas Karamchand Gandhi, *Autobiography: The Story of My Experiments with Truth*, trans. Mahadev Desai (Washington, DC: Public Affairs Press, 1948), 69. For the most useful among the innumerable writings on Gandhi, see Margaret Chatterjee, *Gandhi's Religious Thought* (Notre Dame, IN: University of Notre Dame Press, 1983); Dennis Dalton, *Mahatma Gandhi: Nonviolent Power in Action* (New York: Columbia University Press, 1993); Bradley S. Clough, "Gandhi, Nonviolence, and the *Bhagavad-Gita*," in *Holy War: Violence and the Bhagavad Gita*, ed. Steven J. Rosen (Hampton, VA: Deepak Heritage Books, 2002). For a remarkable compilation of Gandhi's myriad comments on the *Gita*, see Y. P. Anand, *Mahatma Gandhi's 'Works' and Interpretations of the Bhagavad Gita*, 2 vols. (New Delhi: Radha Publications, 2009).

21. Mohandas Karamchand Gandhi, *Bhagavad Gita according to Gandhi* (Berkeley, CA: North Atlantic Books, 2000), xvi–xvii.

22. Ibid., xviii.

23. Ibid., 155.

24. Ibid., xx.

25. Ibid., 58.

26. Ibid., 24.

27. Ibid., 205.

28. On popular notions of Gandhi as an incarnation, see Shahid Amin, "Gandhi as Mahatma: Gorakhpur District, Eastern U.P., 1921–22," *Subaltern Studies* 3 (1984): 1–61.

29. Tapan Ghosh, *The Gandhi Murder Trial* (New York: Asia Publishing House, 1973), 29.

30. Ghosh, *Gandhi Murder Trial*, 303. On Godse's convictions, see also his lengthy trial statement, in Nathuram Vinayak Godse, *May It Please Your Honour: Statement of Nathuram Godse* (Pune: Vitasta Prakashan, 1977). I thank my Bard colleague Sanjib Baruah for urging me to look into Godse and the *Gītā*.

31. Aurobindo Ghose, "Uttarpara Speech," in *Karmayogin: Early Political Writings—2* (Pondicherry: Sri Aurobindo Ashram Press, 1972), 3.

32. Ibid., 4.

33. Ibid., 5.

34. Ibid., 9.

35. Aurobindo Ghose, "On Himself," 37, 34, quoted in Heehs, *Sri Aurobindo*, 70.

36. Aurobindo Ghose, *Essays on the Gita* (Pondicherry: Sri Aurobindo Ashram Trust, 1995), 4.

37. Ibid., 8.

38. Ibid., 10–11.

CHAPTER 5

Modern *Gitas*: Translations

1. Discourse by Jayadayal Goyandka, recorded in Paul Arney, "The Mouth of *Sanatana Dharma*: The Role of Gita Press in Spreading the Word" (paper presented at the American Academy of Religion conference,

Baltimore, November 23–26, 1993). I thank Jack Hawley for sharing a copy of this essay with me. I am grateful to Steven Lindquist for his careful reading of this chapter.

2. Winand Callewaert and Shilanand Hemraj, *Bhagavadgītānuvāda: A Study in Transcultural Translation* (Ranchi: Satya Bharati Publications, 1982). For another useful bibliographic study, see Jagdish Chander Kapoor, *Bhagavad-Gītā: An International Bibliography of 1785–1979 Imprints* (New York: Garland Publishing, 1983).

3. Gerald James Larson, "The Song Celestial: Two Centuries of the *Bhagavad Gītā* in English," *Philosophy East and West* 31, no. 4 (1981): 513–41.

4. Gerald Genette, *Paratexts: Thresholds of Interpretation*, trans. Jane E. Lewin (Cambridge: Cambridge University Press, 1987).

5. J.A.B. Van Buitenen, preface to *The Bhagavadgītā in the Mahābhārata* (Chicago: University of Chicago Press, 1981), xi.

6. Van Buitenen, *Bhagavadgītā in the Mahābhārata*, 5.

7. Ibid., xii.

8. Stephen Mitchell, *Bhagavad Gita: A New Translation* (New York: Three Rivers Press, 2000), 23. Copyright © 2000 by Stephen Mitchell. Used by permission of Harmony Books, an imprint of the Crown Publishing Group, a division of Random House LLC. All rights reserved.

9. Ibid., 32.

10. Isherwood records his efforts to find a suitable translational style in his "Journals of 1942–1943," retold in Christopher Isherwood, *My Guru and His Disciple* (Minneapolis: University of Minnesota Press, 2001, 147–53).

11. Aldous Huxley, *The Perennial Philosophy* (New York: Harper and Brothers, 1945).

12. Nicholas Murray, *Aldous Huxley: An English Intellectual* (London: Little, Brown, 2002), 354.

13. For informative essays on Prabhupada and the founding of ISKCON, see Graham Dwyer and Richard Cole, *The Hare Krishna Movement: Forty Years of Chant and Change* (London: I. B. Tauris, 2007); Steven J. Rosen, *Gaudiya Vaishnavism and ISKCON: An Anthology of Scholarly Perspectives* (Vrindaban: Rasbihari Lal and Sons, 2008). On the publication of *Bhagavad-gītā As It Is*, see Satyaraja Dasa (Steven Rosen), "The Macmillan Miracle," *Back to Godhead* (2008): 24–28.

14. A. C. Bhaktivedanta Swami Prabhupada, *Bhagavad-gītā As It Is* (Los Angeles: Bhaktivedanta Book Trust, 1989), xxix.

15. I am grateful to Steven Rosen and Joshua Greene for their advice on this section.

16. Sarvepalli Radhakrishnan, preface to *The Bhagavadgītā* (New York: Harper and Brothers Publishers, 1948), 5. On Radhakrishnan and the *Gītā*, see Robert N. Minor, "The *Bhagavadgita* in Radhakrishnan's Apologetics," in *Modern Indian Interpreters of the Bhagavadgita*, ed. Robert N. Minor (Albany, NY: SUNY Press, 1986), 147–72.

17. Radhakrishnan, *Bhagavadgītā*, 75.

18. Sarvepalli Radhakrishnan, "The Religion of the Spirit and the World's Need: Fragments of a Confession," in *The Philosophy of Sarvepalli Radhakrishnan*, ed. Paul Arthur Schipp (New York: Tudor Publishing Company, 1952), 7.

19. These are Oppenheimer's own translations of 11.12 and 11.32. Oppenheimer recalled this in a 1954 NBC interview, "The Decision to Drop the Bomb," and in other sources. For a full study of Oppenheimer's engagement with the *Bhagavad Gītā*, see James A. Hijaya, "The *Gita* of J. Robert Oppenheimer," *Proceedings of the American Philosophical Society* 144, no. 2 (2000): 13–32.

20. Buitenen, *Bhagavadgītā in the Mahābhārata*, 117.

21. Mitchell, *Bhagavad Gita*, 138.

22. Prabhupada, *Bhagavad-gītā As It Is*, 399–400.

23. Radhakrishnan, *Bhagavadgītā*, 279–80.

CHAPTER 6

The *Gita* in Our Time: Performances

1. There is no scholarship known to me on oral performances of the *Bhagavad Gītā*. For the best single work on oral performance of Indian religious works, see Philip Lutgendorf, *The Life of a Text: Performing the Rāmcaritmānas of Tulsidas* (Berkeley: University of California Press, 1991). For another valuable work on devotional performative traditions, see Christian Novetzke, *Religion and Public Memory: A Cultural History of Sant Namdev in India* (New York: Columbia University Press, 2008).

2. I am grateful to Shekhar Bajaj, Bharat Mahodaya, and Ashok Mehre for facilitating my visit to Wardha. I also thank Gautam Bajaj and Usha Behn at Paunar Ashram.

3. Mohandas Karamchand Gandhi, "Prayer," in *Ashram Observances in Action* (Ahmedabad: Navajivan Publishing House, 2006), 7–18.

4. The set of prayers are made available in a pamphlet on sale for five rupees at the ashram bookstall: S. P. Pande, *Ashram Prayers* (Sevagram, Maharashtra: Sevagram Ashram Pratishthan, 2006).

5. For his interpretation of the *Gītā*, as a collection of his talks given to fellow inmates while incarcerated in Dhule jail in 1932, see Vinoba Bhave, *Talks on the Gita*, 20th ed. (Paunar, Wardha: Paramdham Prakasham, 2011).

6. Subhash Gethe has published two works on Jñānadeva in English: *Pasāyadāna: The Universal Prayer of Santa Jñāneśvara Mahārāja* (Alandi: Vedanta Swadhyaya Pratishtan, 2007); *Haripāṭha of Sant Jnanaeshvara Maharaja* (Alandi: Vedanta Swadhyaya, 2008). I thank Subhash Gethe for correcting a few errors in an earlier draft of this section.

7. Vishnupant Govind Damle and Sheikh Fattelal, *Sant Dnyaneshwar* (India, 1940). As Christian Novetzke comments, the film depicts Jñānadeva's bhakti as "an activity performed before people, which is in turn projected on a screen and performed for a film-viewing audience." Christian Lee Novetzke, *Religion and Public Memory: A Cultural History of Sant Namdev in India* (New York: Columbia University Press, 2008), 15.

8. Kripananda, *Jnaneshwar's Gita*, 111.

9. A. Parthasarathy, *Śrīmad Bhagavad Gītā*, 3 vols. (Bombay: Vakil and Sons Ltd., 1994).

10. Swami Tathagatananda, interview, New York, April 27, 2012.

11. I thank R. S. Rana for his hospitality at the Sri Krishna Museum and help in answering my questions in an earlier draft of this chapter.

12. Elattuvalapil Sreedharan, personal interview, New Delhi, December 2011. See Swami Vidyaprakashananda, *Gita Makaranda*, 7th ed. (Kalahasti, Andhra Pradesh: Sri Suka Brahma Ashram, 2007).

13. I am grateful to Anil Sutar for responding to my questions concerning the *Shri Krishan Arjun Rath*.

EPILOGUE
THE *BHAGAVAD GITA* IN GREAT TIME

1. Mikhail Bakhtin, "Response to a Question from the Novy Mir Editorial Staff," in *Speech Genres and Other Late Essays*, trans. Vern W. McGee, ed. Carly Emerson and Michael Holquist (Austin: University of Texas Press, 1986), 4.

2. Mikhail Bakhtin, "Toward a Methodology for the Human Sciences," quoted in Katarina Clark and Michael Holquist, *Mikhail Bakhtin* (Cambridge, MA: Harvard University Press, 1984), 348–50.

Advaita Vedānta—nondualist school of orthodox philosophy, especially associated with Shankara

ātman—self or soul

avatāra—incarnation; the "crossing down" of divinity into earthly forms

bhakti—devotion, sharing, or participation in the divine; one of the three paths advocated by Krishna

brahman—universal Absolute, cosmic essence

Brahmin—class of religious specialists, in traditional order of four *varnas* or classes

Devanāgarī—alphabet used in writing Sanskrit and many modern north Indian languages

dharma—harmonious order of things; code of proper conduct; righteousness

jñāna—knowledge, particularly one of the paths or disciplines advocated by Krishna

Kali-yuga—the age of chaos, the fourth era in a degenerating cycle of time, and our current era

karma—action, and moral consequences of action; sacrificial or ritual action; one of three paths advocated by Krishna

Kshatriya—the princely and warrior class, in traditional order of four *varnas* or classes

mārga—route or path; disciplined method

mokṣa—liberation, the highest spiritual aim; freedom from the cycle of death and rebirth

nirvāṇa—liberation; Buddhist term for highest spiritual aim *paṇḍita*—learned person, teacher

prakṛti—source of material world; one of two fundamental categories within Samkhya school

prasthāna-traya—the three textual "points of departure" within Vedanta schools, specifically the Upanisads, *Brahma Sutras*, and *Bhagavad Gita*

puruṣa—person, male; in Samkhya school, the soul or spirit, one of two fundamental categories

śloka—verse form of thirty-two syllables; the most common verse form in classical Sanskrit religious literature

sthitaprajña—the person "whose wisdom is firm," as described by Krishna

Vedānta—the "end" or "culmination" of the Vedas; the Upanisads; name for a group of orthodox philosophical schools utilizing the Upanisads as one of their fundamental texts

Viśvarūpa—Krishna's "all-encompassing" or supernal form, as seen at Kurukshetra by Arjuna

yoga—discipline; Krishna's term for various disciplined means of spiritual advancement

CHRONOLOGICAL LIST

1785 Charles Wilkins. *The Bhagavat-gēētā, or Dialogues of Kreeshna and Arjoon, in Eighteen Lectures; with Notes.* London: C. Nourse.

    First scholarly English translation, in continuous prose.

    Letter of endorsement by Warren Hastings. Translator's preface and notes.

1855 J. Cockburn Thomson. *Bhagavad-gita; or, The Sacred Lay, a Colloquy between Krishna and Arjuna on Divine Matters.* Hertford, UK: Stephen Austin.

    Historical and scholarly orientation. Continuous prose translation with explanatory footnotes.

    Lengthy historical introduction on schools of Indian philosophical thought.

1882 John Davies. *Hindu Philosophy: The Bhagavad gītā, or the Sacred Lay, a Sanskrit Philosophical Poem, the English and Foreign Philosophical Library.* London: Kegan Paul, Trench, Trubner and Co.

    Historical and scholarly orientation. Verse-by-verse prose translation with "philological notes" for each chapter.

    Introduction along with appendix discussing date of text and possibility of Christian influence on its composition.

1882 Kashinath Trimbak Telang. *The Bhagavadgītā with the Sanatsugātīya and the Anugītā.* Vol 8 of *Sacred Books of the East.* Edited by M. Muller. Oxford: Clarendon Press.

> Scholarly orientation. Continuous prose translation with footnotes.

> Historical introduction. Volume also includes two other philosophical portions of the *Mahābhārata.*

1885 Edwin Arnold. *The Song Celestial; or, Bhagavad-gītā (from the Mahābhārata).* Boston: Roberts Brothers.

> Poetic orientation. Verse translation in continuous unrhymed iambic pentameter.

1907 Swami Abhedananda. *Bhagavad Gītā: The Divine Message.* 2 vols. New York: Ramakrishna Vedanta Math.

1938 Sri Aurobindo [Ghose]. *The Message of the Gita.* Pondicherry: Sri Aurobindo Ashram Trust.

> Religious and philosophical orientation. Verse-by-verse prose translation: Devanagari and translation with notes drawn from his *Essays on the Gita.*

1944 Franklin Edgerton. *The Bhagavad gītā.* Harvard Oriental Series. 2 vols. Cambridge, MA: Harvard University Press.

> Scholarly orientation. Verse-by-verse translation in quatrains (corresponding to quarters of Sanskrit shlokas) with Sanskrit text in transliteration on opposing pages. Volume 2 includes lengthy interpretation of *Gita* in historical contexts and Arnold's *Song Celestial.*

1944 Swami Nikhilananda. *The Bhagavad Gita.* New York: Ramakrishna-Vivekananda Center.

> Advaita Vedanta philosophical orientation. Verse-by-verse prose translation with commentary based mainly on Shankara's Advaita commentary. Introduction and brief overview of the *Mahabharata.* Glossary.

1944 Swami Prabhavananda and Christopher Isherwood. *Bhagavad-Gita: The Song of God.* Hollywood: Marcel Rodd Co.

Vedanta and literary orientation. Translation in mixture of verse and prose.

Introduction by Aldous Huxley. Appendixes on cosmology and "The Gita and War" by Isherwood.

1946 Mahadev Desai. *The Gospel of Selfless Action, or the Gita according to Gandhi*. Ahmedabad: Navajivan Publishing House.

Gandhian orientation. Verse-by-verse prose translation: Devanagari and translation with bracketed commentary by Desai adhering to Gandhi's Gujarati translation. Lengthy introduction by Desai. "Anasaktiyoga" by Gandhi.

1948 Sarvepalli Radhakrishnan. *The Bhagavadgītā*. New York: Harper and Brothers Publishers.

Vedanta philosophical orientation. Verse-by-verse prose translation: transliteration, translation, and brief comments.

1967 Maharishi Mahesh Yogi. *Bhagavad-Gita: Chapters 1–6*. London: International SRM Publications.

Religious orientation. Verse-by-verse translation into varied lines of verse: Devanagari, translation, and commentary based mainly on Shankara. Brief introduction. Appendixes on transcendental meditation and other topics.

1968 A. C. Bhaktivedanta Swami [Swami Prabhupada]. *The Bhagavad Gita As It Is*. New York: Macmillan Company.

Vaishnava devotional orientation. Verse-by-verse prose translation: Devanagari, transliteration, word-by-word gloss, translation, and commentary.

1980 Swami Vidyaprakashananda. *Gita Makaranda*. Kalahasti, Andhra Pradesh: Sri Suka Brahma Ashram. First published 1963.

Religious orientation. Verse-by-verse prose translation: Devanagari, transliteration, word gloss, "substance" (translation), and commentary.

1981 J.A.B. Van Buitenen. *The Bhagavadgītā in the Mahābhārata*. Chicago: University of Chicago Press.

Scholarly orientation. Translation in continuous prose with some interspersed verse. Transliterated Sanskrit text on opposing pages.

Translation of several *Mahābhārata* chapters before and after the *Gītā* proper.

Scholarly and historical introduction.

1986 Barbara Stoler Miller. *The Bhagavad-Gita: Krishna's Counsel in Time of War*. New York: Bantam Books.

Combined scholarly and poetic orientation. Verse-by-verse translation in quatrains.

Introduction. Afterword on Thoreau and the *Gītā*.

Glossary of key Sanskrit terms.

1994 A. Parthasarathy. *Śrīmad Bhagavad Gītā*. 3 vols. Bombay: Vakil and Sons Ltd.

Advaita Vedanta philosophical orientation. Verse-by-verse translation: Devanagari, transliteration, word-by-word gloss, translation, and commentary.

2000 Stephen Mitchell. *Bhagavad Gita: A New Translation*. New York: Three Rivers Press.

Poetic orientation. Verse-by-verse translation in loose trimester quatrain.

Introduction.

2008 Laurie Patton. *The Bhagavad Gita*. London: Penguin Books.

Combined scholarly and poetic orientation. Verse-by-verse translation in octaves.

Introduction and extensive list of further readings.

CHAPTER 1.

The *Bhagavad Gita* in the Time of Its Composition

Biardeau, Madeleine. 2002. *Le Mahābhārata: un récit fondateur du brahmanisme et son interprétation.* 2 vols. Paris: Seuil.

Fitzgerald, James L. 1983. "The Great Epic of India as Religious Rhetoric: A Fresh Look at the Mahābhārata." *Journal of the American Academy of Religion* 51 (4): 611–30.

Ganguly, Kisari Mohan. 2004. *Mahabharata of Krishna-Dvaipayana Vyasa.* 4 vols. Delhi: Munshiram Manoharlal.

Hiltebeitel, Alf. 1976. *The Ritual of Battle: Krishna in the Mahābhārata.* Ithaca, NY: Cornell University Press.

———. 2001. *Rethinking the Mahābhārata: A Reader's Guide to the Education of the Dharma King.* Chicago: University of Chicago Press.

Malinar, Angelika. 2007. *The Bhagavadgītā: Doctrines and Contexts.* Cambridge: Cambridge University Press.

Narasimhan, C. V. 1973. *The Mahābhārata; an English version based on selected verses.* New York: Columbia University Press.

Smith, John D. 2009. *The Mahabharata: An Abridged Translation.* London: Penguin Books.

Van Buitenen, J.A.B., and James L. Fitzgerald. 1973–2004. *The Mahābhārata.* 4 vols. Chicago: University of Chicago Press.

CHAPTER 2
Krishna and His *Gita* in Medieval India

Bryant, Edwin F. 2003. *Krishna: The Beautiful Legend of God.* London: Penguin.

Hutchins, Francis G. 1980. *Young Krishna.* West Franklin, NH: Amarta Press.

Krishna Warrier, A. G. 1999. *Śrīmad Bhagavad Gītā bhāṣya of Sri Saṁkarācārya: With Text in Devanagari and English Rendering.* Madras: Sri Ramakrishna Math.

Kripananda, Swami. 1989. *Jnaneshwar's Gita: A Rendering of the Jnaneshwari.* Albany: SUNY Press.

Mainkar, T. G. 1969. *A Comparative Study of the Commentaries on the Bhagavad Gītā.* Delhi: Motilal Banasidass.

Sharma, Arvind. 1986. *The Hindu Gītā: Ancient and Classical Interpretations of the Bhagavadgītā.* LaSalle, IL: Open Court Publishing.

Van Buitenen, J.A.B. 1958. *Rāmānuja on the Bhagavadgītā: A Condensed Rendering of His Gītābhāṣya with Copious Notes and an Introduction.* The Hague: Ned Bock en Steendrukkerij.

CHAPTER 3
Passages from India

Halbfass, Wilhelm. 1988. *India and Europe: An Essay in Understanding.* Albany, NY: SUNY Press.

Herling, Bradley L. 2006. *The German Gita: Hermeneutics and Discipline in the German Reception of Indian Thought, 1778–1831.* New York: Routledge.

Isherwood, Christopher. 1965. *Ramakrishna and His Disciples.* London: Methuen and Co.

Jackson, Carl T. 1994. *Vedanta for the West: The Ramakrishna Movement in the United States.* Bloomington: Indiana University Press.

Robinson, Catherine A. 2006. *Interpretations of the Bhagavad-Gītā and Images of the Hindu Tradition: The Song of the Lord*. London: Routledge.

Schwab, Raymond. 1984. *The Oriental Renaissance: Europe's Rediscovery of India and the East, 1680–1880*. New York: Columbia University Press.

Sharpe, Eric J. 1985. *The Universal Gita: Western Images of the Bhagavad Gita*. LaSalle, IL: Open Court Publishing.

Trautmann, Thomas R. 1997. *Aryans and British India*. Berkeley: University of California Press.

Willson, A. Leslie. 1964. *A Mythical Image: The Ideal of India in German Romanticism*. Durham, NC: Duke University Press.

CHAPTER 4

Krishna, the *Gita*, and the Indian Nation

Desai, Mahadev. 1946. *The Gospel of Selfless Action; or, The Gita according to Gandhi*. Ahmedabad: Navajivan Publishing House.

Gandhi, Mohandas Karamchand. 1948. *Autobiography: The Story of My Experiments with Truth*. Translated by Mahadev. Desai. Washington, DC: Public Affairs Press.

Heehs, Peter. 2008. *The Lives of Sri Aurobindo*. New York: Columbia University Press.

Minor, Robert N. 1986. *Modern Indian Interpreters of the Bhagavadgita*. Albany, NY: SUNY Press.

Nagappa Gowda, K. 2011. *The Bhagavadgita in the Nationalist Discourse*. New Delhi: Oxford University Press.

Subramaniam, V. 1987. "Karmayoga and the Rise of the Indian Middle Class." *Journal of Arts and Ideas* 14–15:133–42.

CHAPTER 5

Modern *Gita*s: Translations

Larson, Gerald James. 1981. The Song Celestial: Two Centuries of the Bhagavad Gita in English. *Philosophy East and West* 31 (4): 513–41.

Page numbers in italics refer to illustrations